Sir John Fortescue's Thunder in the East

Sir John Fortescue's Thunder in the East
The British Army During the
First & Second Burma Wars

J. W. Fortescue

Sir John Fortescue's Thunder in the East
The British Army During the First & Second Burma Wars
by J. W. Fortescue

FIRST EDITION

First published under the title
A History of the British Army (Account)

Leonaur is an imprint of Oakpast Ltd
Copyright in this form © 2015 Oakpast Ltd

ISBN: 978-1-78282-495-4 (hardcover)
ISBN: 978-1-78282-496-1 (softcover)

http://www.leonaur.com

Publisher's Notes

The views expressed in this book are not necessarily those of the publisher.

Contents

The First Burma War	7
Operations about Sylhet, Manipur, and Arakan	60
Burmese Advance from Prome	82
The Second Burma War	109

Chapter 1

The First Burma War

Lord Moira resigned the Governorship-General of India in 1823, and was succeeded after an interregnum of some months by Lord Amherst, son of the conqueror of Canada, who assumed office on the 1st of August. Like Moira he found himself confronted immediately with the prospect of war against a new and untried enemy. On the eastern as on the northern frontier of the British dominions a new power had risen up in the persons of the Kings of Ava, who, after precisely the same fashion as the Gurkha chiefs, had for a full generation been dispossessing the petty chieftains of the country, that is now called Burma, of their territory, and welding it into an empire for themselves.

Assam in the north-east, Cachar, immediately to south of it, and Arakan on the eastern shore of Bengal fell successively into the hands of these conquerors, until their boundaries became conterminous with those of the British; and it was tolerably certain that they would not stop there. The tyrannous rule of the Kings of Ava finally brought about the expected violation of the British frontier.

Thirty years previously in 1793 three Arakanese chiefs, with a rabble of followers, fled across the borders of Chittagong, immediately to west of Arakan, and were pursued by a party of Burmese which had orders not to relinquish the chase whithersoever it might lead them. The governor general at that time, Sir John Shore, remonstrated, but being answered by the Burmese commander with defiance, was too weak and timid to insist upon his withdrawal, and was even abject enough to deliver over the unfortunate fugitives to the tender mercies of the Burmese. The King of Ava naturally concluded that the British were afraid of him, and from thenceforth the tone of the Burmese steadily increased in arrogance.

Meanwhile the oppressed Arakanese continued to swarm over into Chittagong by tens of thousands, in so wretched a condition that it was impossible to refuse them asylum; and the harbouring of these miserable people was made a pretext by the Burmese for a constant menace of war. It was ascertained in 1809 that the Burmese meditated the conquest of Chittagong and even of Dacca, not more than two hundred and fifty miles north-east of Calcutta, so that it was easy to understand why they cherished a ground of quarrel. Moreover, this ground at times became unpleasantly solid.

One of the emigrants in 1811 boldly crossed the border into Arakan with a party of *banditti*, and overran much of the country before he was routed and driven back by the Burmese into Chittagong; and, though the Calcutta government sent a mission to Ava to disavow these insurgents and issued orders for the apprehension of the chiefs, this same leader continued to harry Arakan from time to time until his death in 1815. The cessation of his inroads, however, did not conciliate the Burmese, who, after first sending emissaries into India, ostensibly to purchase manuscripts, but in reality to stir up disaffection, in 1818 openly laid claim not only to Chittagong and Dacca, but even to Murshidabad and Cossimbazar, almost on the main stream of the Ganges. Frequent missions and negotiations served only to bring out the insolent contempt in which the court of Ava held the British. Retaliatory inroads into Chittagong became frequent, and at last the Burmese took the decisive steps which provoked war.

On the 24th of September 1823 they landed a force on the island of Shahpuri, at the mouth of the River Naaf, which had for long been a British possession, overpowered the British guard, several of whom were killed or wounded, and retired.

As Amherst answered this aggression only by remonstrance, the Burmese were confirmed in their belief that the British stood in fear of them. Shortly afterwards two columns invaded British territory, the one advancing from Assam south-westward upon Sylhet, about two hundred and seventy miles north-east of Calcutta, and the other westward from Manipur upon the same point. The former column was attacked and routed north of Sylhet on the 17th of January 1824, by the British frontier-guard, which, however, was too weak to follow up its success; and the Burmese, returning, united with the column from Manipur and threw up stockades east of Sylhet on the River Surma.

Here again they were promptly attacked, and the column from Assam was once more driven back in confusion; but that from Manipur held its own and, beating off the British force, compelled it to retire. Finally, the island of Shahpuri was again seized, and on the 24th of February 1824 Amherst published a declaration of war.

Then the question arose how hostilities could be most successfully prosecuted against such an enemy. Little was known of the country. Two or three British officers had gone on missions to Ava, and one of them, Captain Symes, had set down his experience in a book. A few merchants had also made their way for a short distance up the coast, or up one branch or another of the Irrawaddy, and had seen a few narrow belts of land from the water; but beyond that nothing was known of the geography of Burma.

It was generally understood that the country, or at any rate the southern and more easily accessible part of it, presented the usual features of the delta of a great river within the tropics—continuous tracts of marsh and forest, steaming under a vertical sun, swarming with mosquitoes, unhealthy to the last degree at all times, and subject to heavy inundations during the rains—but beyond this there was nothing save the vaguest of information.

The enemy, moreover, had his own system of warfare, curiously anticipating in some respects that of European nations in the twentieth century, and recalling in others that of the same nations in the seventeenth century. The force consisted chiefly of infantry, of which thirty to forty thousand were equipped with firearms, and the remainder with long spears and short swords; but every man, whether musketeer or spearman, carried a spade or entrenching tool of some kind. Upon arriving in presence of a hostile army, the Burmese troops would take up their ground in good order and, to use a modern phrase, "dig themselves in."

Their system was to delve a succession of holes, each large enough to hold two men and so excavated as to afford them shelter both from the weather and from the fire of the enemy. The line of these holes was designed according to a settled plan, so that it took the form of a more or less continuous entrenchment, in which traverses, as a protection against enfilading fire, were unnecessary, for even a shell falling straight into one of these holes could not kill more than two men.

The actual labour of digging was entrusted in the first instance to the spearmen, the musketeers meanwhile covering them with their fire; and, as the Burmese had no system of reliefs, the whole of the work was done by pairs of men, each hole containing a sufficient supply of food and water for both, and a bed of straw or brushwood under the excavated bank, so that one man could sleep while the other worked, according to the principle known in naval parlance as "watch and watch." In this way an army of tens of thousands would take up its position, and in a couple of hours would disappear underground; and, where they had to deal with a formidable enemy, they would creep up to him, sinking themselves into the earth, for mile after mile.

The spade, however, was only one of their weapons of defence, for a country of dense jungle and forest made the axe equally valuable. The front of a Burmese entrenchment-line was always covered by abatis, skilfully constructed so as to make a most formidable obstacle, and the rear was fortified by stockades, which could either be put together hastily, though strongly, of bamboo, as platforms with loopholes for sharpshooters and with embrasures for light guns, or more solidly built of stout teak beams which defied light artillery. It was a common Burmese

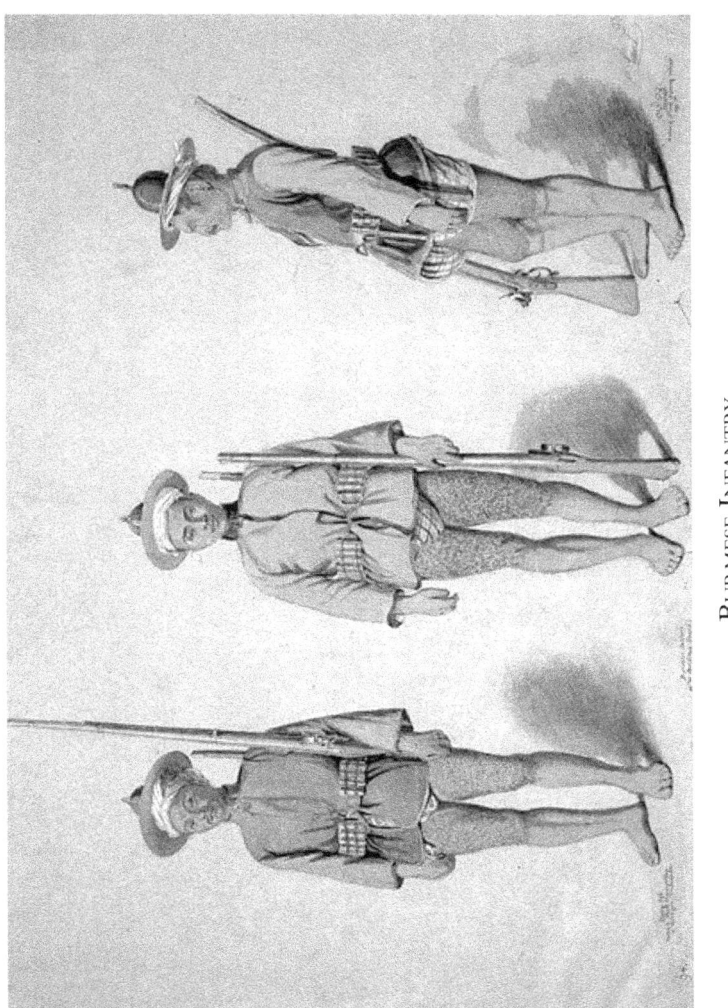

Burmese Infantry

practice also to build platforms in trees, which served as posts of observation and as positions for light guns.

The favourite pieces for this purpose were the small weapons known as *jingals*, which fired a ball weighing from one half to three-quarters of a pound, and were mounted on a light carriage easily manageable by two men. These, having a greater range than a musket and being, in Burmese hands, little less mobile, were weapons to which the British could not easily supply a counter. For the rest the general tactics of the Burmese infantry resembled those of European armies in the seventeenth century, when the musketeers were employed for missile action and the pikemen for shock action. It was the business of the musketeer to keep the enemy from approaching the stockade, and of the spearmen and swordsmen to close with the enemy if he succeeded in entering it.

The musket and bayonet were, of course, supposed to combine missile and shock-action in a single weapon; but even in the twentieth century, when a rifle can be loaded in far less time than a soldier of the eighteenth needed for the mere priming of his flint-lock musket, short clubbing or thrusting weapons have been often preferred for close and crowded fighting in entrenchments. In these circumstances the primitive division of the Burmese infantry into missile fighters and shock fighters was at that time by no means wholly to its disadvantage.

The artillery of the Burmese included a vast number of pieces of various calibres, which, however, were generally used as guns of position, being not readily manoeuvrable, and were frequently brought to the scene of action on the backs of elephants. The cavalry numbered little above seven hundred, and, being drawn exclusively from Manipur, were known as the Kasi Horse. They probably bore a strong resemblance to the English northern horsemen, mounted on tough little ponies, of Henry the Eighth's time.

Such was the country and such the enemy, both very vaguely known and very imperfectly understood, against which the British arms were now to be employed. It was, therefore, unusually difficult to frame a plan of campaign; and the military authorities judged it best to penetrate into the interior of Burma by water only. The Irrawaddy was the great highway. The capital and all of the principal cities were situated upon its banks; and it was thought that, if the proper season were chosen, a flotilla conveying troops could ascend the four to five hundred miles of river from Rangoon to Ava in about six weeks.

In fact it was to be a maritime expedition; and the commander-in-chief, Sir Edward Paget, whom we have known well in the Peninsula both with Moore and with Wellington, could think of no other means for bringing the Burmese to reason. Any military attempt upon the internal dominions of the King of Ava he deprecated, he wrote with picturesque prescience:

> In place of armies, fortresses and cities I am led to believe that we shall find nothing but jungle, pestilence and famine.

It was, therefore, decided that the expedition should arrive at the very beginning of the rainy season, when there would be the greatest possible volume of water in the river; and a naval force was prepared of the *Larne* and *Sophie*, sloops of war, several of the East India Company's cruisers, a flotilla of twenty gun-brigs and twenty war-boats, each carrying one heavy gun, and—wonder of wonders—a small steam-vessel, the *Diana*, the first ever employed in British warfare.

Among the naval commanders was Captain Frederick Marryat, the novelist, and, through his novels, the greatest historian of the Royal Navy during the struggle with the French Revolution and Empire.

The military force was furnished chiefly by Madras, the *sepoys* of the Bengal presidency having an unconquerable antipathy against crossing the sea. Hence Bengal furnished only one detachment of native infantry besides the Thirteenth and Thirty-Eighth of the King's service, while Madras supplied the Forty-First and Eighty-Ninth of the British Line, and the Hundred-and-Second and seven native regiments of the Company's

		Total all Ranks.
Burmese Expeditionary Force :		
Bengal Division. Colonel McCreagh.		
H.M. 13th, 727; H.M. 38th, 1035; 40th B.N.I., 86; European Artillery, 360		2208
Madras Troops. Colonel Maclean.		
1st *Division* : H.M. 41st, 762; Madras Europ. Regt. (102nd), 863; 1st Bn. Pioneers, 552; 3rd Madras N.I., 676; 7th M.N.I., 695; 8th M.N.I., 652; 9th M.N.I., 658; 10th M.N.I., 609; 17th M.N.I., 617; 22nd M.N.I., 711 .		5170
Madras Foot Artillery		560
H.M. 89th (arrived some in June and some in December, 1824)		1012
		10,575
Detachment of Bombay Foot Artillery		69
		10,644

Artillery :
    Light guns—10 six-pounders, 2 three-pounders.
    Heavy guns—6 twelve-pounders, 8 eighteen-pounders.
    Howitzers—2 eight-inch, 4 light five-and-a-half-inch, 2 four-and-a-half-inch.
    Mortars—6 eight-inch, 2 five-and-a-half-inch.

service, (see list following).

The whole formed a body of some eleven thousand men with forty-two pieces of ordnance under the command of Major-General Sir Archibald Campbell, one of the British officers who had gained distinction in the Portuguese service during the Peninsular War. As to transport and supply, everything was left to chance. Since the Burmese were known to be oppressive conquerors, it was assumed that the British had only to appear before Rangoon, at the mouth of the Irrawaddy, to be welcomed as protectors of an enslaved people, who would at once place at their disposal all their resources of food, cattle, drivers, boats and boatmen.

Those who despatched the expedition were, in fact, governed by much the same hopes as was Henry Dundas when he sent Sir Ralph Abercromby to North Holland in 1799. There, in like manner, it was expected that the Orange party would rise and that everything needed would be readily forthcoming; and yet, when Abercromby had forced his landing, he found no support from the inhabitants, no victuals, no boats and no waggons. So soon are the lessons of a great war forgotten.

The rendezvous for the expedition was Port Cornwallis in the Andaman Islands, and there the Bengal division arrived at the end of April, to be joined by the Madras division on the 2nd of May, 1824. Three days were occupied in taking in fresh water; and on the 5th the armament sailed for Rangoon, sending two detachments, the one under Colonel McCreagh and the other under Major Wahab, to seize the island of Cheduba, nearly four hundred miles due north, and Cape Negrais, about a hundred miles north and east, from Port Cornwallis, (McCreagh's detachment, det. H.M. 13th Foot, 7 cos. 40th Bengal N.I; Wahab's detachment, 1/17th N.I., det. Madras Artillery).

On the 10th of May the armament dropped anchor within the bar of the Rangoon River, some fifteen miles below Rangoon city. Lack of wind and the ebb-tide prevented the fleet from going any further on that day; and Campbell had full leisure to arrange his plan of attack. It seemed pretty evident that the arrival of the British was a surprise to the Burmese; and all through the night signal-beacons were observed flaring along the stream to Rangoon to give the alarm. On the morning of the 11th the fleet weighed and continued its way up the river.

After it had covered three or four miles, fire was opened upon it from a battery of two guns, which were promptly silenced by one of the men-of-war; and then there was no further sign of resistance until the ships arrived off Rangoon, when shortly after 2 p.m. a small Burmese battery of twelve guns had the temerity to fire a few shots, and was instantly extinguished by a couple of broadsides from the *Liffey*. Campbell had particularly wished to avoid firing upon the town, as it was of the utmost importance to the British that the inhabitants should remain peaceably within it; but, as it happened, these broadsides delivered from confinement and possibly from death eleven Europeans, inhabitants of Rangoon, who had been secured by the Burmese

The harbour of Port Cornwallis, island of Great Andaman, with the fleet getting under weigh for Rangoon

as hostages. Meanwhile Campbell had made his dispositions for landing; and detachments of the Thirty-Eighth, Forty-First and Thirteenth were set ashore to cover the disembarkation of the rest. These advanced parties met with no resistance; and within twenty minutes the British were in undisputed possession of Rangoon.

Here seemed to be a solid success; but the capture of an oriental city too often means only the beginning of troubles; and so it was in the present instance. Rangoon, upon which the projectors of the expedition had counted for a friendly population with abundance of supplies, transport-animals and boats, was found to be entirely deserted. Upon the first news of the arrival of the fleet at the mouth of the river, the inhabitants had begun to steal away and to hide themselves in the adjacent jungles; less from fear of the invaders than from the persuasion that occupation of Rangoon by the British would be short, and that submission to them would mean no more than to share in their destruction at the hands of their Burmese conquerors.

Abandonment of their homes signified for them hardship and privation during the rainy season in the jungle; but anything was better than the vengeance of the Burmese authorities, who, for their part, with excellent judgment not only permitted but enjoined this flight from the city. There, then, Campbell found himself at the beginning of the rainy season in a wilderness of empty dwellings, surrounded by swamps, which would soon be meres, and by jungles almost as impassable as the swamps, with no means of moving and therefore pinned by sheer force of circumstances to his ground.

The first night spent upon Burmese soil was not creditable to the force. The troops, remembering the booty shared at Seringapatam, looked to enrich themselves by this Burmese expedition; and the sight of the great golden *pagoda* of Shwe-da-gon, towering up, like St. Paul's in London, to a height of four hundred feet, seemed to promise untold wealth in some quarter. No attempt seems to have been made to keep the troops in hand. They wandered away through the deserted streets; and, though they found little plunder, a large party of European troops happened upon a cellar, belonging to an European merchant, full of brandy. In a very short time the party was riotously drunk. The happy news quickly spread to their comrades; and by nightfall the British soldiers, almost to a man, were either prostrate and insensible or rambling, blissfully intoxicated, with lighted torches from house to house, in search of plunder.

The natural result was that half of the town was burned down, and the remainder saved only by the exertions of sailors landed from the fleet; and had the enemy been as enterprising and watchful as they were cunning and provident, they might have annihilated the troops in Rangoon without further trouble. (See *A Sketch of the Services of the Madras European Regiment during the Burmese War* by Major Butler, which is confirmed by Doveton, *Burmese War*).

The officers, as soon as they found out what was toward, sallied out and spilled what was left of the May brandy on the ground; but this measure, which ought to have been taken at first, could not undo the mischief, though probably it at least limited its duration. The entire incident points to negligence and laxity of discipline among the regimental officers, and extreme improvidence, to say the least of it, on the part of the commander-in-chief. Campbell, who had been at Ciudad Rodrigo and Badajoz, must have known the British soldier's passion for alcohol at that period. He must have guessed that liquor was to be found somewhere in Rangoon, and that the men, after long confinement on board ship, would be inclined to break loose in search of it. Not a musket-shot had been fired, and not a drop of British blood had been shed, so that there was no excuse for not keeping the men in hand. In these days of telegraphic communication he might have found himself superseded within forty-eight hours.

On the morning of the 12th May the remaining troops were landed, and Campbell made his dispositions for the holding of Rangoon. The town proper stands on the north side of the river and at that time covered an area of about nine hundred yards

The Burmese Army

by seven hundred, being bordered by shallow water on three sides and by the river on the south side, and being further defended by an inner enclosure of palisades, from ten to twelve feet high. Northward two roads, gradually converging, led to the Shwe-da-gon Pagoda, about two miles and a half distant, passing through groups of substantial buildings, which afforded excellent cover for the troops.

The whole of this line was placed in a state of defence, with batteries thrown up at intervals both to front and rear, and a chain of posts connecting the entire length of it. Headquarters and all departments were stationed in the town, together with the regiments; and the Shwe-da-gon Pagoda was occupied by the Thirteenth and Thirty-Eighth. This building stands upon a mound, which was eight hundred yards square and formed the key to the position. Close up to this line the grass grew high, so high indeed in places that it was necessary to throw up mounds to enable the sentries to see over it, and at all points the jungle was disagreeably near, and so thick as to afford good cover for a skulking enemy.

It was not a highly dignified situation for a British force, landing to punish an aggressive neighbour, but it was inevitable. The desertion of Rangoon by the inhabitants signified that neither land transport and drivers, nor water-transport and rowers, could be obtained; and an army that has no transport must sit still. (The solitary exception to this rule is Sir Alured Clarke's march from Simonstown to Capetown, in 1795).

Very soon it was apparent that the Burmese had thought out their plan of operations with admirable thoroughness, and, having admitted the British into Rangoon, were determined not to allow them to quit it. Under cover of the jungle they threw up earthworks and stockades on every road and pathway, even within musket-shot of the British posts; and from these fastnesses they stole out under cover of night, sometimes firing at the sentries, sometimes creeping up still nearer, hurling their spears at them, and creeping off invisible; at all times lurking on the skirts of the jungle to cut off any unfortunate straggler. Hence, at first the hours of darkness were constantly disturbed.

The men, until they became inured to these wiles, were nervous and unsteady, firing at anything or at nothing and keeping the whole line in a state of alarm. By water also the Burmese had their war-boats, not wholly to be despised by vessels at anchor, and, still worse, their fire-rafts, with which they threatened to drive the shipping out of the river altogether. Meanwhile the enemy, upon which they chiefly counted to make an end of the British, got early to work. Reckoning, upon the reports of a couple of political officers, to find abundant supplies of fresh meat and vegetables, the authorities had sent out the expedition with little more food than was sufficient for the voyage. Of this food the staples were salt pork, at best not the most digestible of meats, and biscuit; and under the influence of the climate the pork turned putrid and the biscuit mouldy.

Dysentery, therefore, declared itself almost immediately; and the weakening of all the men by insufficient nourishment bade fair to offer them as easy victims to malarial fever. It should seem that the Hundred-and-Second, of its own motion, collected some four thousand bullocks, but was ordered by Campbell to release them as being the private property of the natives, whom he wished to conciliate. The officers of course obeyed; but they did not fail to note that Campbell instituted a prolonged, though fruitless, search for hidden treasure in the Great Pagoda, obviously with no intention of restoring it, if found, to its owners; and the men took the hint and proceeded to rifle all the smaller *pagodas* of such small images of gold and silver, worth comparatively little, as they could lay their hands on. Altogether the first weeks of the occupation of Rangoon cannot be considered edifying to the military mind.

It so chanced that operations in another quarter at this same time did much to heighten the confidence of the Burmese. They had assembled ten or twelve thousand men in Arakan under the command of Maha Mengyee Bundoola, an officer of great reputation; and on the 13th of May this force advanced upon Ramu, about ninety miles to north-west of Arakan city, where

View of the Great Dagon Pagoda of Rangoon and scenery adjacent to the westward of the Great Road

Scene upon the Terrace of the Great Dagon Pagoda of Rangoon near the Great Bell.

lay a British detachment of about five hundred Bengal *sepoys* and six hundred irregular levies under Captain Noton. This officer's perfectly correct instinct was to go out and fight; but, owing to the cowardice of his elephant-drivers, his two guns failed him on the day of action, and he fell back to Ramu, where he took up a defensive position and resolved to stand his ground until reinforcements, which were on their way, should join him.

On the 15th of May the Burmese approached him and, by taking advantage of natural cover, succeeded in entrenching themselves close to him. During the night and during the day of the 16th they sapped their way still closer, and by morning of the 17th were within twelve yards of his picquets, upon which they maintained a heavy and destructive fire. Noton's irregulars now abandoned the defence, and, the position being thus rendered untenable, he began his retreat in good order.

The Burmese, however, pressed him hard; and a small body of their horse, cutting down every straggler, filled the *sepoys* with dismay. In spite of all that their officers could do, they gave way to panic, threw down their arms and dispersed. About two hundred and fifty only were killed or taken, but of nine British officers six were killed, and only three, two of whom were wounded, made their escape. Happily Bundoola made no attempt to follow up his success, otherwise he might have mastered Chittagong and Dacca. Reinforcements soon made these secure; but meanwhile there was wild panic in Calcutta, where some of the native merchants actually moved themselves and their families under the guns of Fort William. Altogether the campaign did not open happily for the British.

At Rangoon, however, Campbell and Commodore Grant soon realised that they could not allow the Burmese to have things all their own way; and they began operations on the 19th May by a raid of a company of the Thirty-Eighth, and of the boats of the fleet upon three outlying stockades a little way up the river at Kemmendyne. The Burmese fought well, meeting bayonet with spear, but were driven from all their defences, leaving sixty dead behind them. On the 28th guessing, from the persistent annoyance given by the enemy at one point in his line, that formidable works must be in the vicinity, Campbell led out a stronger party of about two hundred and fifty Europeans and as many *sepoys*, with a gun and a howitzer, to what may be called a reconnaissance in force.

The rain was falling in torrents, which meant that the men, being unable to keep their priming dry, were unable to fire their muskets; and the first two miles of the march lay by narrow paths through dense jungle; so that the enterprise was not without peril. The Burmese, however, fell back steadily, offering now and again an opportunity to the artillery. After advancing seven miles the artillery-men were worn out with the labour of getting their pieces forward; whereupon Campbell, leaving his *sepoys* to protect them, pushed on with his Europeans alone and at length debouched from the jungle into a plain of paddy-fields, some inches deep in water. Two miles ahead stood a village, wreathed in smoke, which seemed to indicate the presence of a large force cooking; and behind it the Burmese officers could be seen drawing up their troops in line.

In high hope of at last meeting his enemy in the open, Campbell pressed on towards the village, just short of which he was met by a heavy fire from two stockades, so cleverly masked as to be invisible at sixty yards' distance. He had in fact been lured on into something very like an ambuscade. With great promptitude he ordered one of his four companies to hold the plain and keep the enemy's main line in check, while he launched the three others to the attack. Fortunately, both stockades were low, not exceeding eight feet in height. In ten minutes the first stockade was cleared with the bayonet; and the troops, re-forming as if on parade, after a sharper struggle carried the second stockade also.

Pursuit was impossible, and Campbell, after waiting for an hour in the hope of engaging the enemy's main force, marched back to camp. His casualties had been trifling, and he had counted three hundred dead of the enemy. It seems that the Burmese system of fortification had one great defect—the outlets in rear of the stockade were always too narrow, so that, when once the

Attacking the stockades near Rangoon by Sir Archibald Campbell, K.C.B., on the 28th May 1824

defenders had ceased to resist, they became huddled together in their flight and were slaughtered without difficulty.

This little affair showed at least that the spirit of the British troops was excellent, and may not have been without its effect on the enemy; but it was not the kind of operation that could be repeated. A march of twenty miles under a tropical downpour is sufficient in itself to send many men to hospital; and the risk of meeting an enemy ten times superior in number with the bayonet alone on difficult ground was very great.

In fact, had the two stockades captured in this day been a few feet higher and had the assault in consequence failed, Campbell's handful of men would probably have been annihilated. On the other hand, nothing succeeds so well as audacity against an oriental foe; and Campbell was assuredly right to put heart into his men, worried as they were through the harassing tactics of the enemy, by taking the offensive. But it is hard upon a commander to place him in such a position that he must accept such risks, or see his army go to pieces.

Before the 1st of June the detachment from Negrais rejoined the main army at Rangoon, having mastered the island with little difficulty or loss but found it not worth the keeping. On the 4th the Eighty-Ninth and two battalions of Native Infantry began to arrive from Madras; and on the nth the detachment from Cheduba, having also accomplished its mission with little loss, came likewise into Rangoon. Their arrival was timely, for sickness was greatly on the increase. Fever was supplanting dysentery; and scurvy and hospital gangrene had made their appearance; nor did it help matters much to ascribe these two last to the " depraved habits" of the men, (Wilson's *Narrative of the Burmese War*).

★★★★★★

In the Third Burmese campaign of 1884-85 the troops were fed chiefly on "bully beef" and biscuit; but I myself saw a case of an officer who, as a consequence of that campaign, developed scurvy some months after his return to England. The symptoms were unmistakable; but the officer in question was not one "of depraved habits," and the disorder was ascribed by the doctor simply to general bad health after two years of fatigue, privation and exposure in a very trying climate. J.F.

★★★★★★

The Burmese during these first days of June sent emissaries to Campbell's headquarters to make a show of negotiation. The object of this could only be to gain time, probably for the assembly of troops to attack the British lines in force; and Campbell was consequently the more intent upon an aggressive policy which should bring their machinations to naught. Petty raids in various quarters had by this time gained for him from fifty to sixty large cargo-boats, which he was adapting for the transport of troops; and meanwhile his attention was specially directed to Kemmendyne, some two miles up the river from Rangoon, where the Burmese had erected one main stockade of unusual strength and extent, with similar though minor stockades in the vicinity. As this seemed likely to be the pivot of the expected Burmese attack, Campbell was anxious to master this stronghold at Kemmendyne; and the commodore was equally solicitous to possess it, since it gave the enemy a convenient station for floating fire-rafts down the stream upon his shipping.

Accordingly on the 3rd of June three columns were set in motion from the Shwe-da-gon Pagoda, two of them under Colonels Hodgson and Smith to converge by different routes upon the great stockade, and a third under Major Frith to a more distant point to intercept the enemy's retreat, while Campbell himself with two cruisers, carrying three companies of the Forty-First, was to come abreast of Kemmendyne by water. Hodgson's and Smith's columns, after a seven hours' march through the jungle, punctually met before the great stockade at noon, together sixteen hundred strong with two camel-howitzers and a rocket-tube-mortar.

The howitzers opened fire with shrapnel, which was not very efficacious against a stout structure of bamboo and teak; the rocket-mortar likewise opened fire with a premature explosion which blew an unfortunate follower to pieces; and presently the flank companies of the Hundred-and-Second advanced to the assault.

The ground all round the stockade was thickly covered with jungle; and, as they moved forward, these companies were greeted by a heavy and regular fire on their rear. Facing about, they returned it, until their commander, judging by the steadiness of the volleys that they were being fired upon by our own native troops, ordered them to lie down. This little mistake having been set right, they flew upon the stockade. It was fifteen feet high, loop-holed and heavily garrisoned; but these gallant men without hesitation tried to storm it by hoisting each other over the top.

They were shot down right and left; but, still undaunted, they tried to pull the stockade asunder by main force. It was too stout for them; and the brigadier, seeing that without scaling-ladders the assault could not succeed, called the men off. They were re-forming for an orderly retreat when the cruisers from the river opened fire, at too great elevation, sending their shot right over the stockade into the middle of the rallying troops. In these circumstances the retirement was not at first too orderly; but the Burmese made no attempt to counter-attack nor to pursue, contenting themselves with yells of triumph. Thus the force, having lost about one hundred and twenty killed and wounded, fifty of them Europeans, returned unmolested to Rangoon.

This was not a fortunate nor a well-managed affair; and the loss of so many European soldiers was a more serious matter than the bare number would seem to indicate. That the British troops should have fired upon each other was nothing extraordinary—indeed in woodland fighting such mishaps are the rule rather than the exception. That the guns of the ships should have played upon their own men in such blind country was nothing very remarkable. But the neglect to provide scaling-ladders, when endless bamboo was to be had for the cutting, was unmistakably culpable, and points to a careless acceptance of unnecessary risks.

Campbell wrote of the whole affair as a reconnaissance which might have developed into the capture of Kemmendyne but for "one or two mistakes," and whose result was little to be regretted "as it would tend to lull the crafty foe into a security that may soon be fatal to him." (Campbell's despatch of 4th June, 1824, printed in Wilson's *Papers*). The term reconnaissance in force, after more than a century of hard usage, still retains its value among the military reports of all nations to disguise the miscarriage of a deliberately planned attack.

On the 6th of June Campbell's losses were made good by the arrival of part of the Eighty-Ninth; and he now planned an attack of Kemmendyne upon very different principles. On the 10th of June he again moved out from his lines against the place, this time with three thousand men, a sufficiency of scaling-ladders, four heavy guns and four mortars, by land; sending up simultaneously two divisions of the flotilla by water. He wrote:

> It was my intention not to lose a man if it could be avoided.

His ordnance could move but very slowly, for the eighteen-pounders, through want of draught-cattle, were hauled along by parties of European soldiers, and the ground was heavy. After five hours of tedious and weary progress the column had traversed two miles, when the way was found to be barred by a stockade stoutly built and fourteen feet high, which was covered on both flanks and in rear by dense jungle. The stronghold was invested on three sides, so far as the jungle permitted; two heavy guns and some field-pieces were brought up, and for nearly an hour the artillery hurled shot, apparently with no great effect, upon the barrier of bamboo and teak.

Campbell then directed strong parties from the Forty-First and Hundred-and-Second to assault the stockade in front, and from the Thirteenth and Thirty-Eighth to assail it in rear. The position was carried with little difficulty or loss; one hundred and fifty Burmese dead being counted, whereas the British casualties did not exceed thirty-two. The force then pushed on at the same snail's pace for another mile, and halted for the night in communication with the flotilla before the great stockade of Kemmendyne.

Campbell made no attempt to surround it completely, alleging, apparently without accuracy, (Butler), that his force was too weak for the purpose; and he spent the night, under torrents of tropical rain, in throwing up batteries. As loud yelling resounded from the stockade throughout the hours of darkness, he felt fairly confident of a decisive affair on the morrow. With the first streak of dawn his guns and mortars opened with shot and shell a fire which was continued for two hours, when the storming columns advanced and found the stockade empty.

The Burmese had evidently decamped during the night, leaving behind them yelling parties sufficient to deceive the British; and not a Burman, living or dead, was to be found within it. The only occupant was one old woman. (Campbell's despatch of 16th June (Wilson's *Papers*), Doveton).

The incident shows that Campbell was but an opportunist commander and had never set himself seriously to solve the problem—certainly no easy one—which was set to him by the Burmese leaders. The ease with which minor stockades had been carried misled him into the careless and somewhat costly attack on Kemmendyne on the 3rd of June; and he was considerably dismayed by his repulse. Experience had shown that, when once British troops had made their way into a stockade, they could slaughter the Burmese like sheep; but merely because on the 3rd of June they had failed to surmount fifteen feet of palisade without scaling-ladders—which was not a very astonishing circumstance—he went round to the opposite extreme and would not attempt an attack without heavy artillery.

The mere labour of hauling heavy guns along marshy tracks at the rate of about four hundred yards an hour must have sufficed to send scores of the British to hospital, especially after exposure in their exhausted state to a night of incessant tropical rain. Moreover, it was found that—as might have been guessed, or at any rate ascertained by experiment—round shot produced little effect upon so elastic a substance as bamboo, the fibres merely expanding to allow for the passage of the ball and closing immediately behind it.

Hence a battering which would have dashed masonry to ruin made a very poor breach in a stockade. Shell was far more efficacious, both in its moral and physical effects, and a few light mortars were therefore worth the trouble of their transport; but the true weapon against stockades, held by such an enemy as the Burmese, was the scaling-ladder. Campbell had plenty of scaling-ladders on the 10th, and, if he had depended chiefly upon them, he would have reached Kemmendyne in infinitely less time and with infinitely less exertion, would have stormed it out of hand, inflicted real loss on the Burmese, and put his men under cover of the huts within the stockades for the night. As things were, he inflicted upon his troops much unnecessary fatigue and exposure—far more costly in the long run than a well-planned assault—and left them with the mortifying impression that they had been outwitted and befooled.

The acquisition of Kemmendyne was, nevertheless, a solid gain, for it gave the British force at least some ground outside the line of its picquets at Rangoon; for, together with the actual town, an almost continuous chain of stockades, extending along the river for nearly a mile above the city, had been abandoned by the enemy. Kemmendyne itself was garrisoned by a native battalion and four companies of the Hundred-and-Second; and an unfortunate detachment of the latter regiment was also posted in the first stockade captured on the 10th. As has been told, nearly one hundred and fifty Burmese had been killed in it; but no pioneers were left with this detachment, nor was a single tool supplied to them to bury the dead. They were fain to burn or inter the corpses as best they could.

The rain soon washed away such slight layer of earth as they had been able to throw upon the bodies; and the troops were left to share the stockade with an unspeakable mass of corruption,(Butler). The result was, of course, an increase of sickness, of which there was already more than enough. Indeed,

The storming of the Lesser stockade of Kemmendyne near Rangoon on the 10th of June 1824

the only excuse for such scandalous neglect seems to be that all departments of the army were more or less paralysed by the excessive prevalence of disease.

The Burmese leaders were evidently well aware of this state of things, for the court of Ava now directed that a general attack should be delivered upon the British lines, and that the invaders should be driven into the sea. The Burmese were probably hastened to this resolution by the capture of Kemmendyne, which was the first indication that their tactics, however successful so far, might fail of their final purpose. They began to resume their old habits of harassing picquets and murdering sentries; and at the end of June large bodies were seen crossing above Kemmendyne from the western to the eastern bank of the river.

On the night of the 25th they floated down a huge fire-raft, consisting of thirty or forty canoes linked together and piled up with faggots, which had been soaked in crude petroleum, for the destruction of the British shipping; but this formidable engine of attack drifted ashore and burned itself out long before it reached Rangoon; and the naval commanders, once aware of this danger, anchored beams in the river to intercept any future fire-rafts. On the 1st of July the expected assault was delivered with such feebleness that it was beaten off easily by three weak companies of *sepoys* and two guns. The British, in fact, suffered not a single casualty.

Still the enemy's force continued to increase, and Campbell, though the monsoon was at its height and much of the country was under water, decided to assail a strongly fortified Burmese post at Pagoda Point, the junction of the Hlaing with the Rangoon River. The main entrenchment was here thrown up on the tongue of land between the two streams; and the access to it was protected by two stockades on either bank of the Rangoon River about half a mile below the confluence.

Campbell himself, with eight hundred men, was to approach it by water, under convoy of the cruisers; and Brigadier-General Macbean with twelve hundred more was to march upon Kamaroot on the Hlaing, about six miles from Rangoon city and a mile and a half above Pagoda Point, to cut off the enemy's retreat. On the 8th of July accordingly the two columns set out. The cruisers easily made their way up to Pagoda Point; and, after a short cannonade, the troops landed, carried two stockades with little difficulty and found a third abandoned by the enemy.

As it was impossible to communicate with Macbean owing to the floods, Campbell returned to Rangoon that evening. Macbean, for his part, struggled through the jungle with difficulty under pouring rain, and soon found himself compelled to leave all artillery, except a few light howitzers, behind. Emerging at length into open ground, he found a series of seven stockades before him. Two of them, though strongly manned, were quickly carried by escalade; and the enemy fell back to a kind of citadel within three separate lines of entrenchments. Here a high Burmese commander had taken up his station; but, though he set a fine example, his men would not stand by him and he was among the first to fall.

Altogether the seven stockades were mastered with ridiculous ease and at trifling loss to the attackers; and the Burmese really suffered heavily, for Macbean, in addition to the enemy actually opposed to him, had the good fortune to intercept a column of fugitives from Pagoda Point. It was reckoned that eight hundred of the enemy were actually killed in these two affairs; and a more refreshing feature was that a combined operation by land and water had actually, for the first time, met with some fair measure of success.

In the lines of Rangoon, however, the situation was ghastly. An officer who had been left in Kemmendyne after its capture, found on returning to the main army, after no more than a week's absence, that the camp was one vast hospital. Europeans, *sepoys* and followers alike were creeping about like ghosts, one and all in the grip of malarial fever. Few seem to have died actually of this disorder; but their strength was so much enfeebled that they fell easy victims to dysentery, scurvy and (though the name was as yet uncoined) no doubt to enteric fever. The mortality was aggravated by the want of the simplest articles of

The attack of the stockades at Pagoda Point on the Rangoon River by Sir Archibald Campbell, K.C.B., 8th July 1824

The position of part of the army previous to attacking the stockades on the 8th of July 1824

diet. There were no milk, no bread, no fish, no fresh meat, no vegetables—nothing but rice, mouldy biscuit and salt pork. The slightest wounds led to mortification—there is no mention of tetanus—and death. The *sepoys*, who suffered a trifle less from malarial fever than the Europeans, had their own peculiar trouble with leech-bite, which developed into hideous ulcers that frequently were only arrested by amputation.

Each of the European battalions had from two to three hundred men in hospital, and each was burying from three to six men a day. The very business of interment was difficult, for the inflow of water forbade the digging of deep graves; and the corpses had to be huddled into a shallow pool, and hastily covered with earth before they could float to the surface. Altogether, there were elements in this Burmese expedition of 1824 which provoke comparison with the worst epidemics of yellow fever in the West Indies, and even with the awful story of Carthagena.

Amid all these afflictions the force did not fall to pieces; and for this, whatever his failings may have been, Campbell deserves the greatest credit. If, through no fault of his own, he could not stay the plague that devoured his army, he at least did his best by constant activity to make the men forget it. On the 19th of July he organised another expedition by land and water to Hlegu, twenty-three miles north of Rangoon, which, however, came to nothing owing to floods which prevented the land force from reaching its destination. From this time forward until October, therefore, operations were confined to the water.

On the 4th of August a flotilla took six hundred men to Syriam, east of Rangoon, where the Burmese had occupied an old Portuguese fort, from which they were promptly driven. On the 8th another small party was sent to the district of Dalla, on the western bank of the Rangoon River, and cleared a couple of stockades there. On the 20th a detachment, consisting of part of the Eighty-Ninth and of the Seventh Madras Native Infantry, was despatched with some vessels of war to reduce the district of Tennasserim, far to the south. This expedition was absent for some three months, during which it captured the towns of

Tavoy and Mergui with little difficulty, and, having left garrisons in these, returned in November to Rangoon.

Meanwhile the main army of the Burmese had fallen back to Donobyu, about fifty miles north and west of Rangoon, evidently disheartened by their many defeats; and Campbell waited anxiously for October, when the rains should come to an end and the inundations should subside. In the course of September three more regiments, (26th, 28th, 30th M.N.I., the 26th arrived on the 1st of October), of native infantry joined him from Madras, doing something to make good his losses from sickness; and, hearing early in October that the enemy's troops in Pegu had moved westward to Hlegu, he sent eight hundred Madras *sepoys*, with two light howitzers, under Colonel Smith to attack them.

On the 5th accordingly Smith moved off, through falling rain and amid intense heat, by a track which was in places two feet deep in water, came upon a stockade after five hours' march, carried it with the usual ease, and learned from a prisoner that in front of him were fighting men of a different description from any that he had yet encountered. Smith therefore halted, and asked for European reinforcements, (Butler).

Campbell refused to send Europeans, despatching instead three hundred native troops. On the 7th Smith resumed his advance, and, after storming a succession of breastworks on the way, came before the main stockade of Hlegu in the evening. Smith being anxious to attack before dark, the place was hastily reconnoitred, without the slightest molestation from the enemy. Not only was no shot fired, but not a voice nor a sound could be heard; and Smith, judging from the intense silence that the place must be abandoned, ordered the scaling-ladders and storming parties to advance without further delay.

Still not a sign of life came from the stockade, and the assailants were no more than fifty yards distant when the Burmese suddenly opened with grape and musketry, firing with such steadiness and regularity in salvoes and volleys as fairly took the stormers aback. The leading ladder-carriers and officers fell, and the *sepoys*, smitten with panic, lay down. Smith hurried up to the head of the column, and, judging that success was out of the question without fresh troops, ordered the men to file away quietly to the rear. This was done without noise or confusion, the howitzers continuing to play on the stockade with great steadiness; but presently panic reasserted itself and the entire party rushed back in a huddled and ungovernable mass.

Happily Smith had still a reserve of two hundred men, whose commander, having heard the bugles sound the retreat, had made dispositions to cover the retirement. The Burmese, as usual, attempted not to improve their success; and, the fugitives having been rallied, Smith fell back without further molestation to his halting place of the morning. His men were more frightened than hurt, their casualties falling below one hundred, few of whom were killed; but two excellent English officers were slain and six more severely wounded.

No sooner had this news reached Campbell than he sent out another force, of smaller numerical strength but containing four Europeans to every three natives, against Hlegu under Brigadier-General McCreagh. This officer marched on the 9th and came before Hlegu on the morning of the 10th; but, preparing to assault on the following morning, found the stockade abandoned. The sight of twenty-three bodies of *sepoys* and pioneers, barbarously mutilated, roused the fury of all ranks; and McCreagh, learning from one or two captured stragglers that the Burmese had retreated to a much larger and stronger stockade, decided to follow them up. His way was obstructed by felled trees and breastworks, but his unexpected advance seems to have struck terror into the enemy, for they fired not a shot, but set fire to their stockade, and ran; and McCreagh was fain to return, pursuit being hopeless.

A raid by water, which started at the same time with Smith's column on the 5th, up the Hlaing River, met with equal success, two very strong stockades being taken with no greater loss than three men wounded. This result was the more remarkable since two of the highest officers of the state of Ava were present, and among the captures was a vast quantity of petroleum accumulated for the service of the fire-rafts. Evidently the Burmese were growing disheartened and more and more unwilling to face the British. They would fire at *sepoys* from behind a stockade, but they flew at the mere sight of the white man with his scaling-ladder.

Altogether the prospect seemed to be improving; and the experience of another distant expedition to Martaban, on the coast a hundred miles east of Rangoon, was still more satisfactory. The military operations, which were committed to Colonel Godwin of the Forty-First with a mixed detachment of his own regiment and of *sepoys*, were of the usual stamp. The expedition sailed on the 13th of October and reached Martaban on the 29th.

The naval officers, in spite of extreme difficulties of navigation, brought their ships alongside; and on the morning of the 30th a seemingly impregnable fort was stormed out of hand by two hundred and twenty men with a loss of twenty-one killed and wounded. The Burmese garrison having disappeared, the inhabitants received the British with every appearance of gratification, showing indeed strong antipathy to the Burmese and offering to make common cause against them. The town of Ye, one hundred miles south of Martaban, was also occupied without resistance, and the British hold upon the Tennasserim Provinces was thereby made the stronger.

Meanwhile the court of Ava had likewise awakened to the need for dealing more energetically with the foreign invaders. For months past reports had reached Campbell that the victorious leader, Bundoola, was moving westward with his army to join a great concentration of Burmese troops at Donobyu; and towards the end of November an intercepted letter from Bundoola himself to the governor of Martaban left no doubt that the British lines would be attacked in force. No news could be more welcome to Campbell, though his army was woefully weakened by disease. In October sickness was more prevalent and the number of deaths greater than in any previous month; and an unusual return of violent rains at the beginning of November retarded the restoration of the convalescent. Scarcely thirteen hundred Europeans were fit for duty at this time, and the native battalions were also greatly enfeebled. On the other hand, since the country was still under water, and even Bundoola's army was moving to its point of assembly chiefly in boats, an advance of the British was held to be impossible until January.

It seems extraordinary that, though Rangoon is but six hundred miles from the mouth of the Ganges, and though the government at Calcutta was, presumably, doing its utmost to supply the wants of the army, Campbell at the end of November was still without land-transport enough to move even a single company, (Snodgrass), and, worse still, without proper food for his men. (A company, it must be remembered, until 1914, did not exceed, as a rule, 100 men; and never kept even that strength for long on active service).

It appears, however, to be a fact that none of the natives in Bengal could be induced to offer themselves for service in Burma. The Bengali is not, at the best of times, distinguished by great courage, and he had been thoroughly terrified by the first mishap at Ramu. There was actually in November a mutiny in a Bengal regiment which had been ordered to the front; and, had not the mutinous spirit been very sternly checked, it might have spread far. Even private speculators did not reach Rangoon with provisions until the later weeks of November, which is some proof that the Government was not apathetic. The prices charged by these speculators were, naturally, far beyond the purses of any but the richer among the officers; but none the less the bare arrival of ships containing such luxuries tended to hearten the troops. (10 *rupees* for a fowl; 30 to 40 *rupees* for a sheep which had cost from 3 to 4 *rupees* in Calcutta—Butler).

It gave them at least some hope that before long there would be something better to eat than the rice—for even the mouldy biscuit seems to have run short—and the salt pork or ham, which had frequently been their staple fare.

★★★★★★

See Doveton, "During this excursion (a week's bloodless expedition to old Pegu) my party had literally nothing to eat but a half-boiled ham and rice for breakfast, dinner and supper, without even a morsel of biscuit." There are worse ways than this of contracting dysentery or enteric fever in the tropics.

★★★★★★

Moreover, five hundred boatmen had come in from Chittagong and were preparing boats for water-transport; and the mere prospect of a more active service tended to raise the spirits of the men.

Upon receiving certain intelligence of Bundoola's approach, Campbell hastened to strengthen his line by the construction of a series of small impregnable posts, fronting both to east and west. For Godwin's force was still absent at Martaban, and another party of the Hundred-and-Second had lately been sent on a bloodless excursion to Pegu, so that, between losses and detachments, his numbers were far too much reduced to enable him to hold two fronts, each two miles long, in any strength. The post at Kemmendyne also was strongly occupied, and was supported on the river by a cruiser and a flotilla of gun-boats, so that the enemy should have no convenient base for an attack on Rangoon by water, nor for floating down fire-rafts upon the British shipping.

By the 30th of November the Burmese Army, said to be fifty thousand strong, was assembled in the forest before the Shweda-gon Pagoda; and a curved line of smoke showed the extent of its bivouacs from the river above Kemmendyne in a southeasterly direction to the Pozundaung Creek. Major Yates of the Twenty-Sixth Madras Native Infantry, who was in command at Kemmendyne, pushed out patrols to his front, and, concluding from their reports that his post would shortly be attacked in force both by land and water, made every preparation for defence. Judging it certain that he would be assailed on all sides simultaneously, he intermixed his Europeans—a mere eighty-seven men of the Hundred-and-Second—with his *sepoys*, to give the latter confidence, and posted his guns—two twelve-pound carronades and a field-piece—on the front towards the river. Before dark his dispositions were complete and half of his men were at their posts, while the others lay down, fully accoutred, and slept by their arms.

The night passed away without a sound, until just before dawn the river above Kemmendyne flared suddenly into light, and raft after raft came blazing down the stream, making the jungle as bright as at noonday. The Company's cruiser, H.E.C. *Teignmouth*, which was stationed above Kemmendyne for the express purpose of checking any attempt to float down fire-rafts and frustrating any menace to the garrison by water, tripped her anchor and drifted down to Rangoon before the conflagration could reach her. The rafts, constantly fed by fresh fuel, glided on; and close in their rear followed a flotilla of war-boats which opened fire upon the stockade, while, ashore, the Burmese swarmed into the jungle, which extended to within fifty yards of the stockade, and surrounded the garrison upon all sides.

Few of them could be seen, and Yates was unable to turn his artillery upon them, needing all his guns to repel the attack of the war-boats. After a short time his fire compelled the Burmese flotilla to sheer off and retire up the river. The fire-rafts ran aground at a bend of the stream and there burned themselves out; and about noon the *Teignmouth* reappeared, having been ordered back to her station by Captain Ryves of H.M.S. *Sophie*. Meanwhile the Burmese troops ashore, despite of the constant fusillade from Yates's soldiers upon their working parties, had dug themselves in and invested the stockade upon every side, pouring a galling fire from their trenches upon the defenders. With sound instinct they had isolated this detached post, and seemed bent upon exterminating the garrison.

But this was only the beginning of Bundoola's manoeuvre. In the forenoon his columns were observed on the west bank of the river moving with great regularity over the plain of Dalla towards the water's edge. The leading division, on reaching its place, flung down its arms and began to throw up entrenchments; and batteries opened fire upon the British shipping, while the main body of Burmese foot disappeared into the jungle in rear. There they too began to entrench themselves and build stockades, gradually reinforcing the first division, as the ground thrown up by it gave shelter to increasing numbers.

Later in the day other troops were seen issuing from the forest a mile before the east front of the Shwe-da-gon Pagoda, from which they extended their line southward to the Pozundaung Creek, within long cannon-shot of the city of Rangoon. This Burmese host flung aside its arms, seized its tools and within two hours had vanished into the earth.

Thus Bundoola's manoeuvre was complete. With his right on the west bank of the river at Dalla, his centre stretching through dense forest from Kemmendyne to the Shwe-da-gon Pagoda, and his left from the Pagoda to the Pozundaung, he fairly surrounded the British force, leaving them only Kemmendyne, the space between their lines, and the channel of the Rangoon river in their rear, that they could call their own. His design was clear enough, namely, to drive the British shipping from the river and, having thus cut off all means of retreat, to overwhelm their army.

It was an ambitious plan, perhaps, and was marred by the fault that the investing line was extended beyond the river, so that there was a dispersion of strength which practically forbade a secret concentration—otherwise easy owing to the jungle—of overwhelming force against a single point. None the less it seems to distinguish Bundoola as no ordinary commander; and the rapidity, order and precision with which his troops took up their ground evoked the hearty admiration of the British staff, (Snodgrass). No European army under the ablest of European commanders could, in their judgment, have done better.

Campbell, who had divined Bundoola's intentions, gladly allowed him to carry them out as the best hope of bringing him to decisive action; and, beyond two highly successful little raids upon points of the enemy's lines near the Pagoda, he made no attempt to molest him. The night passed quietly about Rangoon; but around Kemmendyne, as darkness fell, the sound of gongs summoning the Burmese troops was heard in all directions; and at 8 p.m. the enemy advanced in great force and in perfect silence, to carry the stockade by escalade. The garrison held their fire until the assailants were within thirty yards, and with some trouble beat them off.

No further attack was attempted that night, but firing at small parties, which hovered about to carry off the killed and wounded, continued without intermission till dawn, greatly exhausting the garrison. Moreover, fire-rafts were once again sent down the river, followed up by war-boats; and for the second time the *Teignmouth* deserted her station and dropped down the river, leaving to the defenders of Kemmendyne the duty of defending the post on the side of the water as well as of the land.

When daylight of the 2nd broke, the Burmese were found to have pushed their trenches to within fifty yards of the stockade, whence, safe under cover, they poured a very steady and accurate fire upon the British. Yates, now sorely pressed both from land and water, was presently somewhat relieved by the gallantry of Lieutenant Kellett of the king's sloop *Arachne*, who made his way, in the face of hundreds of Burmese war-vessels, up to Kemmendyne and, realising the situation, brought up three gun-boats which swept the assailants of the stockades away with showers of grape.

The *Teignmouth* also returned, under orders, to her station, where she engaged the Burmese war-boats at some disadvantage, for their guns outranged hers. Yates then shifted one of his carronades into the remains of a small building on the front face; but the gunners had not fired more than two rounds before they were shot down, and he was obliged to withdraw them. There was in fact no safe shelter within the stockade even for the wounded, for the Burmese marksmen, ensconced in trees, commanded every corner; and the fire from their entrenchments was incessant and steady throughout the day.

Soon after dark the enemy again attacked with the greatest courage and determination, carrying scaling ladders and evidently bent upon mastering Yates's stockade. Twice they were beaten off, and twice they rallied and returned to the assault, but after a third repulse, having suffered very heavy loss, they would try no more, but merely harassed the garrison by constant feints with small parties. Simultaneously with this onslaught by land, a mass of fire-rafts again came down the river, followed by war-boats; and once more the *Teignmouth* dropped down the river, leaving Kemmendyne to its fate. Captain Chads, the senior naval officer, therefore, sent up H.M.S. *Sophie*, together with three gun-boats, as well as the *Teignmouth*, to ensure proper naval protection, and the *Sophie* took up her station early on the 3rd.

The Burmese now brought their fire-rafts down close to the British vessels, with their war-vessels firing over them to keep the British boats at a distance, and did not set light to them until the last moment. Even so, however, they failed to touch the Sophie, and, though the *Teignmouth* was kindled, (Report of Captain Chads, R.N., Wilson, *Papers*), for a short time, the fire was extinguished before she had sustained any damage. In the course of the day the Burmese war-boats, finding that their guns were of longer range than the British, became very bold, and Captain Ryves thought it well to plan a surprise attack upon them.

Accordingly at dawn three man-of-war's boats and six gun-boats under Lieutenant Kellett made a dash into the midst of them, captured seven, and drove the rest in panic up the river. This was a most gallant feat, for Kellett's craft were all of them small and his force did not exceed seventy men, whereas the Burmese boats were some of them as much as eighty feet long, were heavily manned, and carried a nine-pounder in the bows, (*ibid*).

In spite of their many repulses, however, the Burmese still pressed Kemmendyne hard. Their fire from the trenches was continuous and harassing, and they brought up to their trenches two light guns which gave much annoyance. On the night of the 4th they once more attacked with as great resolution and daring as ever, returning to the assault again and again, but without success; and from that time forward, though they never intermitted their fire, they lost heart and energy, for, as must now be told, the Burmese had suffered defeat also before Rangoon.

Though the detachment sent to Pegu had rejoined him on the 2nd, Campbell attempted no serious operation until the 5th, wishing, according to his own account, that the enemy should bring his full force and the whole of his reserves forward so that his defeat might be the greater. On the 4th he ordered Captain Chads's flotilla to enter the Pozundaung Creek and cannonade the enemy's left rear at daylight, and prepared two columns, the one of six hundred men under Major Walker, the other of eleven hundred men under Major Sale of the Thirteenth, to attack the Burmese centre and left respectively.

The assault of the infantry, delivered at 7 a.m., was immediately and easily successful; and a troop of the governor-general's bodyguard, which had arrived on the previous evening, made some havoc of the Burmese in the pursuit. Bundoola thereupon joined the remnant of his defeated left and left centre to the troops which were threatening the Shwe-da-gon Pagoda; and Campbell, to lull him with false security, ceased fire with his artillery and kept his infantry out of sight.

Encouraged by these signs, the enemy sapped up closer and closer to the British defences, with loud boastings of defiance. At 11.45 a m on the 7th Campbell suddenly opened a heavy fire from every gun that he could bring to bear on the hostile entrenchments, and at noon assaulted with four columns of infantry. The attack was instantly successful; and the Burmese were driven off with heavy loss, leaving over two hundred pieces of artillery—the bulk of them light swivel-guns—and a great number of muskets behind them. The affair put an end to the Bundoola's grand design; and his retirement was not so well executed as his advance, for, after the withdrawal of the main body, he still left his right detachment in isolation at Dalla, from which it was driven on the 8th with considerable loss.

On the 9th the investment of Kemmendyne was raised, and the entire Burmese force was in retreat. The casualties of the British between the 30th of November and the 9th of December were under two hundred and fifty, of which not thirty were killed. There was, in fact, no very severe fighting except at Kemmendyne, where the little garrison was really hard pressed, beating off constant attacks and being continuously under fire with little rest or sleep for a week. The Twenty-Sixth Madras Native Infantry, (now the 86th Carnatic Infantry), carries the honour of Kemmendyne upon its colours to this day; and, though it is doubtful whether they would have lived to earn it without the help of the few score of the Hundred-and-Second who were intermingled with them, the defence of the stockade was creditable to both regiments.

For the moment Campbell was so confident that he had defeated Bundoola's army decisively that, on the evening of the 7th, he is said to have made the parole "victory" and the countersign "complete." From the pompous and bombastic tone of his despatches he was quite capable of such little theatrical displays as this; but he very soon found out his mistake. Bundoola, as a matter of fact, retired no farther than to Kokein, four miles north of the Shwe-da-gon Pagoda, where he rallied his army and, having received reinforcements, entrenched and stockaded himself "with a judgment in point of position" (to use Campbell's own words) "such as would do credit to the best-instructed engineers of the most civilised and warlike nations."

Moreover, his spirit was not in the least daunted, and he was resolved to resume the offensive. The information of a deserter led Campbell to expect an attack on the 14th; and in fact fire-rafts were sent down the river on that day, though to no purpose. On the same night the city of Rangoon was kindled in several quarters by Bundoola's emissaries, and great part of it, including the quarters of the Madras commissariat and several private stores, was destroyed. This blow was a shrewd one, for the army was just receiving proper supplies and transport for the first time, and wholesale destruction of this kind could not fail to throw all arrangements into confusion.

Campbell responded by moving out on the 15th in two columns, the right of five hundred and forty men under Brigadier-

General Willoughby Cotton, who had lately arrived, and the left eight hundred strong under his personal command; the former being designed to work round to the rear of the Burmese Army, while the latter should attack in front. The enemy's position was exceedingly strong, consisting of a large stockade upon either flank connected by a central entrenchment, and occupied, as was reckoned, by twenty thousand men. Upon coming up before it, Campbell fired signal guns, which being duly answered by Cotton, he launched his troops in two divisions to the assault of the stockades, while Cotton assailed the centre from the rear.

In twenty minutes the position was mastered and the enemy in full flight. Bundoola was not present in person, but the Burmese, apparently, were so confident that they made no attempt to fire against the frontal attack until the stormers had reached the ditch before the stockade. Cotton's column was more severely tried, having several strong entrenchments to carry before they reached the main work; and the Thirteenth in consequence lost eleven officers and fifty-one men slain or hurt, Majors Robert Sale and Dennie, afterwards famous in Afghanistan, being both of them among the wounded. But even so the total of the casualties did not exceed one hundred and thirty-six. During the engagement the indefatigable Lieutenant Kellett attacked the enemy's flotilla by water, and by skilful manoeuvring of the *Diana*, steamboat, captured thirty war-boats and several fire-rafts.

This action finally extinguished the Burmese hopes of driving the British from Rangoon. The remnant of the defeated army fell back to Donobyu, leaving posts only on the Hlaing and Panhlaing Rivers to harass the British advance. For the character of the war was now to be changed. Transport both for land and water was at last arriving, and the British, after being cooped up for some eight months at Rangoon, were preparing to march to Ava.

CHAPTER 2

Operations about Sylhet, Manipur, and Arakan

With the retirement of Bundoola's army to Donobyu, the entire aspect of Rangoon was changed. The wretched inhabitants, much thinned by forced labour at stockades and entrenchments, and by every kind of ill-usage, instantly swarmed back into the city. In a few days a bazaar was opened, and gradually fresh meat and vegetables made their appearance, at first in small quantities but later in abundance. Beef their religion forbade the Burmese to sell, but they had no such scruples as to live buffaloes. The men took service readily as servants and drivers with the commissariat, and also as rowers, though at first the number of boats was small and far from adequate to the needs of the army.

The troops were cheered also by the arrival of transports with reinforcements. The Forty-Seventh Foot, additional horse-artillery including the rocket-troop, more squadrons of the Governor-general's bodyguard and, best of all, seventeen hundred draught cattle, all came in during the last days of December and first of the New Year. The low ground of the delta was still so wet that it was not considered feasible to advance until February, nor was it expected that, in the few months before the monsoon should set in, the advance should be carried beyond Prome, less than halfway to Ava. But it was hoped that even the defeat of the army at Donobyu might suffice to bring the court of Ava to accept terms from the British.

For the operations of 1825 were not to be confined to the valley of the Irrawaddy. An army of some eleven thousand men, including two King's and six native regiments of infantry, (see list following), besides irregular levies, had been prepared and placed under the command of Brigadier-General Morrison for the invasion of Arakan; and a naval force of small vessels, including one steamship and some eighty gun-boats, was to accompany it.

Morrison's force:

2nd Local Horse	621
Artillery	667
1st Brigade—H.M. 44th, det. 26th B.N.I., 49th B.N.I.	1809
2nd Brigade—H.M. 54th, 42nd and 62nd B.N.I.	2416
3rd Brigade—10th, 16th M.N.I.	1062
2nd L.I. Bn.	1033
Native levy	553
Pioneers	649
7th, 14th, 39th, 44th, 45th, 52nd B.N.I	2399
	11,209

It was thought possible that Morrison might be able to cross the range of mountains that separates Arakan from the valley of the Irrawaddy, and join hands with Campbell. Yet again, a force of about seven thousand men, including six regiments of native infantry, had been collected under Brigadier-General Shuldham on the Sylhet frontier, with the idea that it should penetrate by Cachar into Manipur and thence threaten Ava from the north. Lastly, a corps of three thousand men, comprising two regular native battalions under Lieutenant-colonel Richards, had ever since the end of October been engaged in clearing the Burmese out of Assam.

With the operations of Richards, which, though most exhausting to his troops, amounted practically to the hunting down of cowardly *banditti*, we shall not concern ourselves. It must suffice that by the end of January Richards, thanks to the exertions of a few very efficient British subalterns, had well completed his task, though some of the wild tribes continued to give trouble during the summer.

Shuldham's operations, as may be supposed, were not so successful. He had nothing to dread from the enemy but much from the climate, and from the tangle of torrents, mountains and dense forests through which he was expected to advance. With immense labour his pioneers, covered by about a thousand native levies, in the course of January cut a rude pathway through the forest for a certain number of miles. In February the rain began to fall in frequent heavy showers; the soil became miry and transport almost impossible. Hundreds of bullocks, many camels and even elephants were lost in the endeavour to keep only the advanced guard and the pioneers supplied; and in March Shuldham gave up the enterprise as hopeless.

The dethroned Rajah of Manipur then begged to be allowed to do the work alone with his own levy of five hundred men, armed by the British; and after a march of three weeks from Sylhet he reached Manipur and drove out the Burmese with little difficulty. Thus the work was effectively done; but all the expense of assembling and equipping Shuldham's force was absolutely thrown away. The Calcutta Government had evidently decided upon this expedition without the slightest knowledge of the country.

The story of Morrison's expedition is far more tragical. His force was assembled at Chittagong as early as September 1824, but was detained until January 1825 by the protraction of the rainy season and the old difficulty of collecting transport and supplies. A road had been made from Chittagong to the mouth of the Naaf river, about one hundred miles to the south; and Morrison, leaving Chittagong at the end of January, began his march southward, his flotilla carrying his supplies parallel with him by sea. Upon reaching Cox's Bazar, about eight miles from Ramu, he had to decide whether he should bend eastward, turning the heads of several waters which lay between him and Arakan, and then wheel south upon the city, or whether he should pursue his way down the coast and cross those same waters where they became formidable obstacles, near their mouths.

As to the former course, it was extremely doubtful whether there were any road; and it was certain that the way led through a wild country of mountain and forest through which possibly men might penetrate, but loaded animals, or in other words ammunition and food for the men, certainly could not. Moreover, a great proportion of his transport-cattle had not even joined him. As to the latter, the traversing of broad estuaries—for such the waters became, whether Morrison knew it or not—might take a long time, but at least the supplies could accompany the force and the troops would not starve. Morrison accordingly decided to follow the coast.

On the 1st of February he reached Tek Naaf, about eight miles from the river's mouth, and sent a detachment across it to Maungdaw, on the eastern bank, where no enemy was seen and the population was friendly. The main body was then likewise passed over the estuary, a distance of five miles; but this operation was naturally tedious, and it was the 12th of February before Morrison was able to move, even then leaving much of his baggage on the western bank and many of his cattle still on the road from Chittagong to Tek Naaf. From Maungdaw there was a road of some kind to Arakan, for the Burmese had retreated by it; but Morrison determined still to march along the coast, apparently for the old reason that he was still short of land transport. He therefore left one of his brigadiers at Maungdaw, with the equivalent of two batteries and two squadrons, giving him orders to follow him as soon as cattle equal to the conveyance of three weeks' supplies should have crossed the Naaf, while he himself pursued his way to the river Mayo, half of his force moving by land and half by sea.

The former reached the Mayo on the 22nd of February, but

the detachment at sea met with a violent storm which compelled them to return with the loss of some boats and baggage though of not a single life. Eventually they reached the Mayo on the 27th of February; and the force was gradually brought up a network of creeks to the mouth of the Arakan Branch, up which lay the way, navigable for the most part, to Arakan. These movements were not completed until the 20th of March, nor were the troops ready to resume their advance before the 24th.

The line of march lay along the eastern bank of the river, the road plunging down constantly into the beds of tributary watercourses and up over low ridges parallel with them. The troops were healthy; the climate was not unfavourable; the people were friendly; supplies were abundant, and it seems that the transport-cattle had at last reached the army. (I infer this from the fact that Brigadier-General Richards, who had been left at Maungdaw to bring forward the transport cattle, had rejoined the army).

After two days spent in crossing these difficult tidal watercourses and reconnoitring the passes into the hills, the force was on the 26th distributed into three columns and a reserve, and began the ascent of the hills. Here at last the enemy appeared at the first crest, but they were easily driven from their entrenchments; and the passage up the river was opened for the flotilla, which, a month earlier, had been repulsed in an attempt to ascend it. On the 27th there was again some resistance, easily overcome; on the 28th the force halted to allow the rear to close up, and on the 29th the enemy's main position came into view on a range of rugged hills, strongly entrenched, and held by about nine thousand men with several pieces of artillery.

One pass alone led through these hills to Arakan; and at this point Morrison attacked with eight light companies supported by six battalion-companies. So steep was the ascent, however, that the assault was beaten off, chiefly by large stones rolled from the summit; and, after several officers of the storming column had fallen wounded, Morrison called off his troops and abandoned the attempt. (Morrison in his despatch says that all the officers were wounded, but his casualty-list belies him).

Having observed that the right of the enemy's position, being of great natural strength, was weakly held, he turned his attention to that quarter, and, after a day spent in bringing up his heavy artillery, began to construct batteries during the night of the 30th to play upon the defences of the pass. At daylight of the 1st of April the guns opened fire, continuing all day; and at night the defences of the Burmese right were assaulted and carried without the loss of a man. With some difficulty a gun was brought up to the captured point to silence a troublesome Burmese piece, and then, upon the mere menace of an advance upon their right flank, the Burmese took to flight. They were pursued, but only one formed force, about three hundred strong, was overtaken and destroyed by the irregular cavalry, the remainder having dispersed. The British casualties from the 26th of March to the 1st of April were under two hundred, the number of the killed not exceeding twenty-three.

Having secured Arakan city, Morrison on the 8th of April detached the equivalent of three battalions under Brigadier-General Macbean by water to Ramree and Sandoway, off Cheduba Island, both of which places were occupied without resistance; and thus, so far as the deliverance of Arakan from the Burmese was concerned, Morrison had completed his work. There remained the far more difficult task of carrying his troops over the hills to eastward to form a junction with those of Campbell.

Between Arakan city south-eastward to Dalet, at the foot of the mountain-chain which separates Arakan from Ava, lay some seventy miles of low jungly ground seamed by many waters, not wholly impracticable, perhaps, for the march of a small force, but difficult and uncertain. Of the country from Dalet eastward, little or nothing was known then and not a great deal seems to be known even now; but it was certain that the passage over the mountains, if possible at all, would be a most arduous undertaking, over rough and precipitous heights where baggage and guns could not be brought forward without immense labour and much delay, where supplies did not exist and where even water was difficult to find.

Moreover, the old difficulty of transport-cattle was still present. Even in June not a bullock had yet crossed the Mayo River, while some were still north of the Naaf; and, when Arakan fell, there can have been few that had reached even the Mayo. Lastly, the extremely slow progress of the force in its movement from Chittagong to Arakan left little time for operations before the breaking of the monsoon.

In these circumstances, Morrison decided to form a small exploring column about one thousand men strong, (Light companies of H.M. 44th and 54th. 16th Madras N.I. 3 cos. of 2nd Bengal L.I.), which he placed under command of Major Bucke, and sent by water to Dalet. The regular trade-route between Arakan and Ava ran from An, about twelve miles to south-east of Dalet; and it is not clear why this was not selected, for the fact must have been known to the military authorities, and Bucke actually sent an officer to make inquiry in that direction. (See his report to Morrison, 27th May, 1825, in Wilson, *Papers*).

However, he proceeded to Dalet, arriving there apparently on the 16th or 17th of May, and on the 19th made a short advance of four and a half miles, all the way up a steep ascent. On the following days the march was still more arduous, over range after range of mountains; and it is fairly evident that the road, or path, can have been traversable only in single file, occasionally widening to admit two men abreast; for, though the advanced guard reached its halting-place at 11 a.m., the main body and baggage did not come in until night.

On the 22nd the little column was fain to halt. Many men had fallen sick; many cattle had perished; and both troops and beasts were enfeebled and fatigued to the last degree. On the 23rd another harassing march increased the sick-list; but there was now definite information that a hostile post lay upon the road at the next halting-place; and Bucke laid his plans for surprising it by a night attack.

Before nightfall, however, his native scouts came running in with the news that the enemy lay astride the road only a few miles ahead. One of the guides had been shot, two more had been captured; and the Burmese were apparently in two distinct parties, their strength unknown and unascertainable. In the circumstances Bucke decided to retreat. His force was so much diminished by sickness, and those fit for duty were so much weakened by toil and hardship that they could hardly have withstood an attack, much less have delivered an assault after a long and exhausting march. It is probable that he did wisely. The rains had already begun, and were in full strength before he could return to Arakan; and it seems that the majority of Bucke's detachment fell sick of malarial fever and died.

The fate of Morrison's main body may as well be related at once, so that the operations in this quarter may be done with and dismissed. With the breaking of the monsoon in May, fever and dysentery broke out virulently among the troops in Arakan; and shaken as they were, by the fatigues and privations even of a few months of active service in the tropics, they fell down by hundreds. The climate, indeed, was sufficiently trying.

During July, August and September the thermometer ranged from ninety-two degrees to seventy-eight degrees Fahrenheit; and no one who has not felt a sudden fall of temperature, even if only from eighty-five degrees Fahrenheit to seventy-eight, during tropical rains, can have any idea what it means. The rainfall, too, was terrific, amounting to one hundred and three inches in July and August alone; and this of course signified, for one thing, much confinement of the men within doors, with nothing to do, and, for another, perpetual steaming heat which took all strength and energy out of them and played havoc with the biscuit and salt provisions upon which they subsisted. Not unnaturally they flew to alcohol, which seems to have been abundant, to kill the monotony and discomfort of such an existence, and thereby undermined such physical stamina as the climate had left to them.

Between May and September the European soldiers, altogether about fifteen hundred strong, buried two hundred and fifty-nine men; and the native troops, out of a total strength of about eight thousand, lost nearly nine hundred. Furthermore, at the end of September there were nearly four hundred English and over thirty-six hundred natives in hospital. Officers suffered little, if at all, less than the men, and Morrison himself, being invalided home, died on the voyage. The end of the rains seems to have brought little change; and at last, after eight months' stay in Arakan, the remnant of the force was withdrawn and distributed among less unhealthy stations, to recover itself. In those eight months the Forty-Fourth and Fifty-Fourth, with an average strength of a thousand men, lost close upon six hundred dead; and not half of the survivors were alive at the close of another four months.

These losses, as also those at Rangoon, being incurred on active service in the course of a campaign of aggression, provoked greater attention than at ordinary times they would have attracted. They were not really more serious than the British garrison and the British navy had suffered in the West Indies for more than a century, with hardly a word said. As Sir George Beckwith had truly remarked, a British battalion in the West Indies even in peace required to be renewed every two years; and the fact was accepted as more or less inevitable. Nevertheless, the Government of India seems to have gone to work somewhat blindly in planning this invasion of Burma from the eastern shore of the Bay of Bengal, with either very imperfect knowledge, or very unwarrantable defiance of the nature of the country and of its climatic conditions. But the truth is that the chief authorities of the Company's service and the Company's army had little idea or experience of a campaign except one of the old-fashioned kind in the plains.

The wars in Nepal and Central India had taught them something, but not much; and the occasion demanded a livelier imagination than is common, saving among really great statesmen or commanders. There seems to have been a tendency to blame Bucke for want of enterprise; but four days' march appears to have reduced his detachment to such a condition that another week's advance would have left it helpless to move either forward or back. Morrison, again, has been censured because he moved by water instead of by land upon Arakan; but his chief reason for so doing seems to have been that he felt uncertain of his ability to feed his troops if he moved by land; and it is difficult not to admit that it was cogent.

The only modern parallel that I can remember to the task imposed upon Morrison is the advance upon Manipur in March 1891, when some three hundred British troops, (4 companies of 4/60th), having been brought up the Irrawaddy by water, entered the hills nearly three hundred miles north of Arakan, and made their way unopposed some fifty miles, as the crow flies, to the summit of the range. Their transport consisted of pack-mules, which are preferable to pack-cattle; they were dressed in khaki of sensible cut, and not in the red *coatee* with the oppressive cross-belts, in which the Forty-Fourth and Fifty-Fourth took the field, and they had good protective helmets. Their food was good biscuit and "bully-beef," and, their numbers being only one-third of Bucke's, the column was so much the shorter and the fatigue so much the less. Yet even so the men were sorely tried.

The path was so narrow that they could rarely move except in single file, and that mules, losing their footing, fell over precipices and were dashed to pieces. The heat was so great that three men died in the first day's march, and water was so seldom to be found that the soldiers could not be kept from quenching their thirst from foul, stagnant pools. The natural result was much sickness; and indeed it should seem that nothing, even in these days, can prevent such campaigns from taking a heavy toll of human life. It is easy to condemn our ancestors for thoughtlessness and foolhardiness in undertaking such an adventure at all; but it must be remembered that they were a century younger in experience than ourselves.

For carrying the war to a successful issue, therefore, everything, though as yet he could not be aware of it, turned upon Campbell and the force in the valley of the Irrawaddy. In the course of January he had received as reinforcements the second battalion of the First Royals, and, apparently, a new battalion of

Madras Native Infantry also, (38th).

His shortest route to Ava was by Pegu and Toungoo, on the line now taken by the Burma State Railway, a distance of from three hundred and fifty to four hundred miles. This would have enabled him to turn the whole of the Burmese positions on the Irrawaddy and upset all their plans of defence; but he had not even now land-transport sufficient for such a movement; and he accordingly resolved to make the river still his main line of supply and to advance in two parallel columns, the one by water, the other, even with it and at no great distance, by land. Since this left the parallel valley of the Sittang untouched, the Siamese, who were in name, at any rate, our allies, were requested to advance upon Toungoo, though there was no very sanguine hope that they would do so.

The land-column, of which Campbell took personal command, was limited to thirteen hundred British infantry, a thousand *sepoys*, two squadrons of cavalry, one troop of horse-artillery and the rocket-troop. The land transport was insufficient even so to carry more than a fortnight's supplies, and then only through the sacrifice of every comfort by both officers and men.

This force was to advance parallel to the Hlaing River and, after driving away the enemy's posts that lay upon that stream, was to join the marine column at some point below Donobyu. This marine column, which was commanded by Brigadier-General Willoughby Cotton, was to pass up the Panhlaing channel, expel the enemy from their stockades at Panhlaing and then, entering the main stream, was to push on straight to Donobyu. It included only eight hundred European infantry, with a small battalion of *sepoys* and a powerful train of artillery, and was embarked in sixty river-craft, every one of which was armed with at least one gun. It was accompanied by an escort of boats, manned by one hundred seamen, from the men-of-war lying at Rangoon.

A third column, consisting of the Thirteenth Foot and the Twelfth Madras Native Infantry, was embarked in transports under Major Sale for the reduction of Bassein, nearly one hundred miles west of Rangoon upon another branch of the river. It was hoped that, after the capture of Bassein, Sale might find land-transport enough to enable him to join the rest of the force at Donobyu or at Henzada, thirty miles to north of it. It will be observed that even now, ten months after the departure of the original expedition, Campbell could not collect transport enough, by land and water combined, to advance with more than four thousand men.

On the 11th of February Campbell's column moved off through the jungle, passing, just beyond Kemmendyne, some miles of stockading which had been thrown up for the purpose of checking the British advance, and had been since abandoned. During the first three days not an inhabitant was seen, but on the fourth day a village of the primitive tribe of the Carians was reached and the people were found to be thoroughly friendly. They gave information of a certain force of the enemy five miles ahead; and Campbell laid his plans for surprising this party next day, but was disappointed by its immediate and precipitate flight.

Progressing slowly, for his cattle were still weak, Campbell on the 23rd reached Hlaing, and halted to replenish his waggons from provision-boats which had followed him up the river. Here for the first time since leaving Rangoon the country was found to be well stocked with buffaloes, which afforded a good supply of fresh meat but were found useless for purposes of transport, being unable to endure the sun for the shortest march. Exhilarated by this novel experience, and by native reports that Bundoola had neither the troops nor the spirit to hold Donobyu against a resolute attack, Campbell seems from this moment to have abandoned his original idea of uniting with the marine column before that position. Instead of turning west, he headed north. His column now entered the great teak forest, 24th, and moving by easy stages struck the Irrawaddy at Tharrawaw, some thirty miles to north of Donobyu, on the 2nd of March.

Practically not a shot had been fired so far; and the most trying experience of the troops had been weary night marches along narrow paths through dense, dark forests, the men in single file holding on to each other's clothes lest they should lose the track, which even the native guide could with difficulty follow.

On the 1st of March Campbell had received a message from Cotton that he had captured Panhlaing and was moving up the Irrawaddy. Campbell answered by a brief order to Cotton to send boats down the river to bring up further supplies for the land-column, and halted to expect the arrival of the marine column. For four days he waited with great and increasing anxiety. To his intense mortification he had reached Tharrawaw just in time to see the entire population landed on the other side of the river, the people having deserted the place and carried off practically all boats.

Native reports agreed persistently that Bundoola had withdrawn his troops from Donobyu westward, some said towards Bassein, some towards Arakan, in either of which cases Campbell was on the wrong bank of the river and could not hope, with the few canoes that he had collected, to pass his division across it in less than a week. He had some idea, it seems, of marching direct upon Prome, which was the grand object of the campaign; and he might very likely have reached it with his own column, unaided, and with no more than trifling loss. But it was useless to advance to Prome unless he were sure that the navigation of the Irrawaddy were free and open behind him, for he depended upon water-transport for the subsistence of his troops.

Lastly, he had filled up his waggons from his floating magazines for the last time on the 1st of March; and, since those waggons only carried fifteen days' supplies, he grudged every day's halt, for it compelled him to consume a day's food to no purpose, and every day's food so consumed diminished his chance of forcing a decision in the few weeks that remained before the breaking of the monsoon. Such are the cruel difficulties imposed upon commanders by governments which give them troops but no adequate means of moving them.

At last on the morning of the 7th heavy firing was heard to southward. It lasted until 2 p.m., when it entirely ceased. Natives came in with report upon report of Bundoola's total defeat, and

Campbell heard them willingly, for the news was that which he longed to receive. Every consideration dictated an immediate advance to Prome, the condition of his supplies, the importance of reaching it before Bundoola's defeated army, and the hope of doing so before the country on his immediate front could be laid waste. None the less, he thought it prudent to await yet another day some message from Cotton; and, since no such message arrived and accounts of Bundoola's retreat continued to stream in, he left a strong detachment at Tharrawaw and on the 9th resumed his advance.

On this day and the 10th he marched altogether twenty-six miles, finding all towns and villages deserted and everything that could be of use to him carried away. There was no sign of hurried or confused flight; on the contrary everything pointed to a pre-arranged and systematic denudation of the country such as Wellington had counted upon, under Portuguese law, in his retreat to Torres Vedras. Soon after dawn on the nth the long awaited despatch from Cotton came in. His attack upon Donobyu had failed, and without strong reinforcements he could not hope to carry the position.

The river column had duly embarked on the 16th of February and made its way up the river, destroying a few stockades as it went, and arriving before Panhlaing on the 18th. Here there were three stockades, two in advance, one on either side of the river, and the main stockade of Panhlaing itself a mile above them. In the course of the night the Burmese sent fire-rafts down the river, with no effect, and on the following morning Cotton reconnoitred the works and made his dispositions.

As the ebb-tide forbade the armed vessels to come up until late, Cotton threw up a battery of four mortars and two field-pieces before the advanced works, and formed a column of assault upon each bank of the river. The bombardment aided by the fire of the rocket-battery speedily drove the Burmese out, and by evening the whole of the works, including the main stockade at Panhlaing, had passed into Cotton's hands at the cost of two casualties. He then proceeded to remodel the main stockade for his own purposes, to keep open the communication by the river.

This detained him for five days, and on the 25th he resumed his advance up the river. On the 26th the flotilla reached shallow water, which necessitated the unloading of the heavier vessels; and, owing to the delay thus caused, it was not until the morning of the 6th of March that the armament cast anchor about two miles below Donobyu. Going forward by water to reconnoitre the place, Cotton found that he was confronted by a succession of stockades gradually increasing in strength until they culminated in a kind of citadel upon commanding ground, surrounded by a deep abatis and the usual accessories of Burmese fortification. The place appeared to be crowded with men and defended by several guns. At 1.30 p.m. Cotton sent in a flag of truce to summon the chief to surrender the place within an hour; and at 3.30 p.m. he received a civil but resolute message of defiance.

Two courses lay open to him: either a frontal attack parallel to the river upon the whole depth of the enemy's defences; or a landing above the citadel and an attack upon it from the rear. The latter was that which commended itself to him; the more so because there were good artillery-positions to cover the disembarkation of the attacking troops. But he judged himself to be too weak for such a venture. His battalion of native infantry had been left at Panhlaing; eight of his flat-boats had been sent down to the same place to bring up provisions, in compliance with Campbell's order; and it was therefore imperative to guard the river carefully, so far as that point, until the convoy should return.

Small detachments and sickness had left but six hundred of his seven hundred and fifty Europeans at his disposal for action. If these could be kept together, it was nothing beyond their power to capture a fortified position defended by twelve thousand Burmese; but the naval commander was of opinion, no doubt correctly, that, if Cotton landed above Donobyu, one half of the force would be needed in the boats to keep open the navigation of the river below. Bundoola had been taking pains to train his artillery, and the fire from his river-batteries was steady and accurate. The Burmese war-boats were not by any means contemptible. On one occasion already they had dared, though unsuccessfully, to take the offensive; and Bundoola by his tactics in the past had shown that he knew how entirely the invaders were dependent upon their communication by water for their hold upon Burma.

Rightly judging that to divide his tiny force would be to ensure failure, Cotton had no alternative but to deliver a frontal attack, leaving the flotilla to defend the river. Accordingly on the 7th he landed five hundred bayonets a mile to south of the Burmese position, and advanced in two columns, the Eighty-Ninth on the right, and detachments of the Forty-Seventh and Hundred-and-Second on the left, against the outermost of the stockades, covered by the projectiles of two six-pounders and of a small rocket-battery.

The enemy opened a heavy but not very destructive fire, which they maintained to the last with unusual perseverance. It seems that the two columns attacked the flanks of the work, or one of them the front and the other the rear, for after forcing an entrance they intercepted the retreat of many of the garrison and, besides killing many with the bayonet, captured nearly three hundred prisoners. The casualties of the British in this assault did not exceed twenty; and Cotton prepared for the attack of the next stockade, which was five hundred yards from the first, and at about the same distance from the citadel. Two more six-pounders, four mortars and additional rockets were brought up; and, after these had played for what was deemed a sufficient time upon the enemy's defences, two hundred men of the Forty-Seventh, Eighty-Ninth and Hundred-and-Second advanced in two parties to the storm.

The Burmese opened a heavy fire which caused the columns to swerve from the designated point of attack, and the British found themselves in a ditch, filled with bamboo spikes and under the full blast of the Burmese shot. Officers and men did all that they could, but their losses were so heavy that Cotton called them off. Five officers and about one hundred men—that is to say at least one half of the storming party—had been killed or wounded, and Cotton, realising that, even if he carried the second stockade, he would be too weak to capture the citadel, re-embarked his men without loss or molestation on the 8th, and dropped down the river to his position of the 6th. (Cotton's report of 9th March 1825; Wilson, *Papers*; Butler).

Such was the unpleasant story which reached Campbell on the 11th. He had no one but himself to thank for it; for it was he who had altered his original plan of meeting Cotton before Donobyu, and thrown upon Cotton the whole burden of forcing this strong position, the capture of which was essential to the maintenance of his communications. He had now only ten days' supplies for his column in hand; and he could not count upon the country to feed his troops even for a day.

The people fled everywhere before him, and if by chance he caught some straggling inhabitant he could obtain nothing from him but the awe-stricken cry of "Bundoola." The truth was that the Burmese commander had outwitted Campbell. He had so terrorised the inhabitants that they would do nothing but by his order, and say nothing but that which he wished to be believed. There was nothing for it but to fall back and join Cotton before Donobyu, and on the 12th accordingly Campbell began his return march, reaching Tharrawaw on the 13th. Now came the task of passing his division across the Irrawaddy, which was both wide and rapid, with no better craft than a few small canoes.

This operation took five days and nights of unceasing work; and it was not until the 18th that headquarters were established on the western bank at Henzada. Here a report came in from Sale at Bassein. Sale had come before that place on the 3rd of March and found it burned and deserted, the garrison having retired up the river. Sale followed them up by boat with a small party; and Campbell, hearing that they were encamped fifteen miles away, detached a column under Colonel Godwin at nightfall to surprise them. The march of this column was instantly detected and reported by beacon-signals to the Burmese camp, and Godwin upon reaching his destination found that the enemy had vanished. Sale, therefore, returned to Bassein and took no further part in the operations.

Two days, the 19th and 20th, were consumed at Henzada in re-loading the transport-waggons; and on the 21st Campbell resumed his march southward. On the 22nd his pioneers had to cut a path for nearly ten miles through a tangle of tall grass and reed, from ten to twenty feet high; and on the 24th he came within sight of Donobyu, about four miles distant. On the river above the stockade lay a fleet of war-boats, which promptly turned out to cannonade Campbell's reconnoitring parties; and there was every sign that Bundoola was both ready and confident. On the 25th Campbell moved up within long cannon-shot of the main stockade, which we have called the citadel, and found that it extended along the river for nearly a mile, with a breadth varying from four to eight hundred yards.

The stockading was of solid teak beams, from fifteen to seventeen feet high, planted firmly in the earth as close together as possible, strengthened by cross-beams, and provided with banquettes. Behind this wooden wall rose old brick ramparts; and the ground was honeycombed with subterranean excavations for protection against shell-fire. A wide deep ditch, full of spikes, holes and other impediments surrounded the defences; outside this again were several rows of strong palisades; and outside this once more was an abatis thirty yards broad. The garrison was reckoned at fifteen thousand men, Bundoola's best troops, with one hundred and fifty guns and swivels.

Such a stronghold was too extensive for investment by Campbell's small force; and, the ground on the north-west face and most of the eastern face being open, he took up a position with his left on the river and his right curved round towards the centre of the eastern face. While the troops were in motion the enemy's guns fired continually, but, when once the camp had been pitched, they fell suspiciously silent. At 10 p.m., just as the moon was setting, Bundoola made a feint attack upon Campbell's left and centre, directing his principal effort to the turning of the exposed British right. The two battalions on the right of the line, changing front to their right, easily checked these Burmese attacks, which were finally beaten off at a cost of little more than twenty casualties; and by midnight all was again quiet.

On the 26th Campbell sent a detachment of three hundred men by a wide detour to open communication with Cotton. With the help of three elephants this party forced its way through the jungle without firing a shot, but, when it tried to return, it found the thicket strongly occupied by the Burmese and prudently remained with Cotton. On this same day the enemy's war-boats were driven from their anchorage by the discharge of a few rockets, and ground was broken at a convenient point about three hundred yards from the enemy's entrenchments.

On the 27th the British flotilla came up the river, passing by the stockade under a very heavy fire but suffering very little damage.

★★★★★★

Snodgrass says that on the 11th of March Campbell's column had not ten days' supplies left; he adds that the navigation of the Irrawaddy was so completely commanded that not a canoe could pass the stockade at Donobyu. He also says that no communication was opened with Cotton's column until the 26th, which can only mean that no boats came up the river. How Campbell's column was fed between the 20th and the 27th, therefore, seems to be something of a mystery. Presumably ten days' supplies means ten days' full rations, and the troops received but half.

★★★★★★

Bundoola promptly directed a sortie against Campbell's right, his cavalry and seventeen war-elephants, each of which carried a proportion of armed men, heading the attack. These were charged by the governor-general's bodyguard. The Burmese cavalry were easily routed; and the drivers of most of the elephants were shot, with the result that the sagacious animals turned round and walked back with staid deliberation into the stockade. Bundoola, as was afterwards reported, was so furious at the failure of his artillery to sink the British flotilla that he cut down two of his gunners with his own hand.

On the 28th the steamship *Diana* and some smaller craft succeeded in taking nine of the enemy's warboats; on the 29th, Campbell, having already constructed his batteries, began to get his guns into them; and on the 1st of April his mortars and rockets opened fire. On the 2nd the breaching batteries likewise opened, at daylight; but almost immediately afterwards two Bengali *lascars*, who had been prisoners in the stockade, ran out bringing the tidings that Bundoola had been killed by a shell on the previous day, and that the entire garrison had dispersed during the night. Reconnaisance soon proved the news to be true. So instant and so hasty had been the flight of the Burmese that they had not removed a single gun nor even destroyed their stores of grain. Thus one lucky shot had given Campbell possession of Donobyu, together with over one hundred and thirty guns and over two hundred and fifty wall-pieces, at no dearer price than seventy casualties. Above all, it had delivered him from Bundoola.

This chief, as it seems to me, is entitled to our respect. By sheer force of character he had kept his half-disciplined troops together, and had surrounded them not only with a circle of devastation but with a veil of impenetrable secrecy. As a tactician no doubt he failed before Rangoon; and, although his position and field-works at Donobyu would, in the opinion of Campbell's staff, have done credit to the most scientific engineer, it is objected with some force that he would have done better to hold the narrow channels of the Panhlaing and the Hlaing instead of the main stream of the Irrawaddy, where the ground was in part open plain, well suited to European manoeuvres.

Still, as regards the essential points of denying to his enemy supplies and land-transport and doing his utmost to drive the British from the water, he showed sound judgment; and his efforts, not wholly unsuccessful, to improve his artillery show that he could not only formulate a correct military policy but could think out the means of executing it. The mere fact that his men, deaf to the entreaties of his junior officers, simply melted away after his death, testifies to the strength of his will and the sway of his moral ascendency.

On the night of the 3rd Campbell left Donobyu with the Thirty-Eighth and Forty-Seventh, reached the bank of the Irrawaddy opposite Tharrawaw on the 7th, and, with the help of the boats of the king's ships, passed them over the river before nightfall. The rest of the force followed on successive days, with the exception of the Hundred-and-Second and three hundred and fifty *sepoys* which were left to occupy Donobyu; and by the 12th the whole were on the eastern bank of the Irrawaddy at Tharrawaw. On the 14th Campbell reached the point from which he had turned back a month before, heading for Prome, and prosecuting his advance received on the 19th a Burmese messenger from that city, who represented the desire of the court of Ava to terminate the war by treaty.

Campbell answered that he would be prepared to negotiate when he reached Prome, and continued his march. On the 24th, when within eight miles of Prome, he received a second envoy, who suggested, in not too civil terms, that the negotiations should be opened in the space between the opposing armies. Campbell answered that the military occupation of Prome could not be dispensed with, but that he would be ready to meet the Burmese emissaries next day to arrange for the protection of the inhabitants and of their property.

Before daylight on the 25th his force was in motion, and on arriving before Prome found a very formidable line of defence prepared but abandoned, and the city itself in flames. It appears that the negotiations had been opened only with a view to gain time; and, as Campbell had refused to halt, the Burmese had as usual destroyed everything that could be of use to him and had retreated, laying waste the villages on their way and driving the people into the jungle.

All hopes of ending the war before the rainy season now

vanished. The Burmese troops, thoroughly demoralised it is true, were rallying at Minhla, some eighty miles farther up the river, and might possibly be again dispersed; but to reach Ava, over two hundred miles away, before the breaking of the monsoon was out of the question. Campbell therefore resolved to canton his troops at Prome and to use the few remaining weeks of the dry season in clearing the district of banditti, and in pushing a detachment as far as possible in the direction of Toungoo, a hundred miles to eastward. This column penetrated no farther than to the foot of the Galadzet mountains, about forty miles to east of Prome, when the rains compelled it to return.

Meanwhile the troops settled down at Prome; and the inhabitants, receiving assurance of protection and of liberal payment for their produce, soon returned to the city and rebuilt it. The villagers also, no longer coerced by the defeated armies of Ava, streamed back into the deserted provinces to the south and settled down to work. In a very short time, thanks to the excellent discipline of the troops and the indulgent good nature which invariably characterises the British soldier, comfort and abundance reigned in Prome; and, more important still, it was possible to turn the place into an advanced base for the next campaign. Large fleets of canoes appeared on the water; droves of the finest oxen issued from the jungle; carts and drivers were readily forthcoming.

The Burmese civil magistrates were reinstated, with some limitation of their authority; and the people settled down to order and prosperity. The troops were happy and fairly healthy. At any rate, if they fell sick they were not nourished on food which was as good as poison to them. It was a pleasing contrast to the last rainy season at Rangoon that at Prome there died not more than one man in seven of the British soldiers.

CHAPTER 3

Burmese Advance from Prome

The court of Ava spent the rainy season in collecting troops from its northern states, and by the end of September, 1825, had raised a new army of seventy thousand men, which at that time began to assemble at Meaday, about forty miles to north of Prome. Campbell earlier in the month had sent a letter to Ava setting forth the ruinous consequences to the king if war should be prolonged, and in October he received a conciliatory answer. Negotiations were, therefore, opened at a point halfway between Prome and Meaday; an armistice was declared; and, after many days of discussion, the negotiators parted with every appearance of a favourable issue.

But the British had hardly returned to Prome when reports were received that predatory bands of the Burmese army had broken into the neutral zone demarcated by the armistice, and were laying waste the country up to the very gates of the city, cutting off supplies from Rangoon and threatening the vital communication of the British with the sea. The entire Burmese host then advanced upon Prome in three divisions, their right upon the west bank of the Irrawaddy, their centre on the eastern bank, and their left about ten miles to east of the river, on the farther side of a belt of dense forest, and therefore isolated from the other two. In addition to these there was a reserve of ten thousand men in a strongly fortified position at Minhla, and two detached forces, the one ready to oppose any movement from Arakan, and the other in the neighbourhood of old Pegu, more or less menacing Rangoon.

The effective force at Prome at this time was six weak British battalions, numbering altogether about twenty-eight hundred of all ranks, and seven native battalions with a total strength of rather over three thousand of all ranks, besides a good proportion of artillery and a troop of the governor-general's bodyguard. At Rangoon there was a garrison of about three thousand, chiefly native troops, and at old Pegu were stationed the Hundred-and-Second and three battalions of *sepoys*.

Donobyu had been evacuated in August, the defences having fallen to pieces in consequence of the rains, and the troops there had been brought up to headquarters. On the whole, after providing a sufficient garrison for Prome itself, Campbell could count upon a field-force of about five thousand men, perhaps three-fifths of them Europeans.

About the 10th of November the left division of the Burmese Army under Maha Nemiao, a veteran officer who had been charged with the general direction of the operations, took post at Wettigan, about sixteen miles to north-east of Prome, threatening to turn Campbell's right and to sever his communication with the south. Campbell on the evening of the 15th accordingly ordered four battalions of native infantry, under Colonel Macdowell of the Madras army, to drive the enemy from this post; one battalion being designed to hold them in front whilst the three others assailed their left flank.

The Burmese, having evidently been exactly informed of the plan of operations by their spies, came out to meet the column halfway, and engaged them in a running fight through the jungle, bringing forward cavalry to threaten them wherever the thicket gave place to open ground. Thereby Campbell's combinations were utterly upset.

Two battalions seem to have blundered upon the stockades of Wettigan at different times from different quarters, but, being unsupported, were beaten off. It is impossible to understand the details of the confused fighting that ensued; but the general result was that Macdowell fell early, shot through the head, that the entire enterprise went to wreck, and that the various battalion-commanders drew off their men as best they could. One column, being pursued, had to fight its way back through the jungle, harassed by musketry from three sides; and the four battalions returned to camp in the last stage of exhaustion, having lost over two hundred killed and wounded, and among them no fewer than twelve British officers.

This was a bad beginning for Campbell's new campaign; and Maha Nemiao, without abandoning his threats against the British communications, ordered a general advance upon Prome. Campbell was obliged to send out detachments to clear raiders away from the east bank of the river fifteen miles below that city, and to establish a post of two hundred men at Padaung, about eight miles to south of him on the western bank, with a division of the flotilla to support it. Maha Nemiao had evidently found out that Campbell was expecting reinforcements and treasure to join him, and was doing his best to intercept them.

His attempts were, however, foiled by the resolution and gallantry of Captain Deane of the Royals, who was in command at Padaung, aided by the indefatigable Lieutenant Kellett of the Royal Navy; and in the last days of November a part of the Eighty-Seventh, together with the rest of the convoy, arrived at Prome, having lost no more than two men killed and one officer wounded by the fire of the enemy from the bank.

The main body of the Burmese Army had meanwhile been creeping steadily nearer, stockading itself anew at every mile of its advance. Maha Nemiao's division, opposite the British right, had reached its halting-place on the Nawin River, and, veiled by the jungle, was working assiduously to strengthen a position which could not be seen and about which nothing could be discovered. The central division was in full sight of the eastern bank, fortifying the heights of Napadi, no more than five miles away; and the right division was as busy upon the western bank.

To quote the words of a staff-officer, (Snodgrass):

Every day now produced a change in the Burmese line; each morning discovered to us some new work in front of where their advanced parties had been posted on the previous evening.

Moreover, Maha Nemiao had with him eight thousand Shans from the Chinese border, who had never yet been beaten by the British, and were encouraged by the presence of three handsome young women, prophetesses endowed by magic with invulnerability, who had risen up among them with predictions of a speedy victory. In spite of all previous defeats there was still good spirit in the forces of the King of Ava. They did not realise, as the British staff had instantly perceived, that their three divisions were not within supporting distance of each other.

Having received his reinforcement, Campbell at once laid his plans for an attack on the 1st of December. The flotilla, now under command of Commodore Sir James Brisbane, was to open at dawn a cannonade upon the enemy's posts on both banks of the river, and a body of *sepoys* was at the same time to advance along the margin of the river upon Napadi. This feint was to draw the enemy's attention to his right and centre, and meanwhile the true attack was to be delivered upon his left. Accordingly, at daylight the force, less four battalions of *sepoys* which were left to guard Prome, moved out in two columns, the right under Cotton, taking the direct road north-eastward to Simbike, a few miles up the Nawin River, while the left, under Campbell in person, crossed the stream lower down, and worked up its right bank in rear of the hostile position.

They were hardly under way before the sound of Brisbane's cannon told that the flotilla had begun its work; and Cotton, upon reaching the enemy's line, found that even their picquets had been withdrawn to meet the expected attack upon Napadi. As usual the Burmese position was well chosen and very strong. The stockades were erected upon an open space with dense jungle upon either flank, and were skilfully designed to bring a cross-fire to sweep the front, by which alone they could be approached. Cotton divided his column into two parties, one consisting of five light companies, (of H.M. 1st, 41st and 89th; and of the 18th and 28th Madras N.I.), and the other of the

Forty-First, and launched them straight at two different points. The Shans stood firm until the British entered the stockade and closed with them; and then all resistance collapsed and gave place to wild panic.

Old Maha Nemiao and a few grey-haired chiefs stood nobly and fought to the last, but their men rushed away to the rear of the stockade, where, the outlets being too few and narrow, they were bayoneted by scores. So speedy was the British success that Campbell's column had not time to get fairly into the rear of the fugitives, though his horse-artillery was able to work great havoc among them as they crossed the ford of the Nawin, and effectually to head them back from joining the centre division, if indeed they ever thought of such a thing. Maha Nemiao was found dead, and the corpses of his faithful attendants, who had tried to carry him away, lay by his body.

One of the prophetesses was mortally stricken; another was either wounded or frightened out of her senses by a shell while fleeing across the ford; and the third was not. The left division of the Burmese host had been utterly defeated and dispersed. Losing no time, Campbell, after giving his troops two hours' rest, brought them back to the ford of the Nawin which he had crossed in the morning, and from which a path led to the position of Napadi. He also sent orders to Brisbane to be ready to co-operate in the projected attack of the morrow. The last of his troops did not reach their bivouac until after dark, worn out after some fourteen hours on foot in tropical heat.

At dawn on the 2nd they were in motion again, Campbell's detachment filing along a narrow path through the jungle, and Cotton's seeking a way farther to the north by which he might strike the flank and rear of the Burmese position. Cotton was instructed that he should attack at whatever point he might reach in the enemy's defences, and that the sound of his firing should be the signal for Campbell's men to assail them in front.

After two hours' march Campbell's column debouched upon a plain by the river, opened communication with the flotilla, and halted before the stockaded heights of Napadi. The Bur-

41st Regiment of Foot

mese position was peculiarly formidable. So far as can be ascertained by description, it lay in a bend where the river turns from a southerly to a south-easterly course. Within this bend stood three ranges of hills, the foremost commanded by the second, and the second by the third. The enemy's right flank was securely covered by the river, his left flank as securely by dense forest.

At the foot of the foremost hill, itself very steep and rugged, and fortified at the base by three stockades, was a belt of jungle overlooking a strip of beach nearly a mile long—evidently a former bed of the river—and beyond the beach ran the river itself. The only possible ground from which the main position could be attacked was this same beach; and it was necessary to seize it without delay. Six companies of the Eighty-Seventh therefore fetched a compass through the forest, came in upon the flank of one of the stockades and of the belt of jungle, swept the enemy out of it, and cleared the beach to the base of the foremost hill. The troops then occupied the captured ground; the flotilla moved up the river, firing heavily upon both banks; and Campbell waited anxiously for the sound of Cotton's musketry to launch his assault.

He waited long in vain, so long that at last he formed his troops for the frontal assault in despair of any help from Cotton, first detaching the Forty-Seventh Foot and the Thirty-Eighth Madras Native Infantry under Colonel Elrington to penetrate, if possible, through the jungle on his right and effect at least some diversion on the enemy's left flank. Just as the storming column was moving off, Elrington made his presence felt; and the Thirteenth, Thirty-Eighth and Eighty-Seventh first captured the two stockades at the base of the foremost hill, and then very deliberately marched up the hill itself, without deigning to answer the enemy's fire by a single shot.

Having scoured this hill with the bayonet, they proceeded to clear the next and in due time the third also, until they had mastered the entire position, nearly three miles in depth. The flotilla, meanwhile, seized the opportunity to push up the river past the defences, and captured all the boats and stores of the Burmese Army. Cotton's column had found it impossible to make its way through the forest and had been compelled to return, but Campbell's alone was sufficient for the work. Thus the enemy's centre was routed and dispersed with heavy loss, and the whole of his guns, supplies and stores were taken or destroyed.

There remained the right division on the western bank of the Irrawaddy; but so closely were the Burmese hidden from observation that it needed forty-eight hours to discover whether they were still holding their ground or whether they had retreated, leaving only a rearguard in the stockades. Having satisfied himself that they were still in position, Campbell on the night of the 4th established a mortar-battery and a rocket-battery on an island within good range of the stockades. On the morning of the 5th these opened fire upon the riverward front of them, while the infantry, landing higher up the stream, fell upon the left flank and rear. Disheartened by the defeat of their comrades of the central division, the Burmese after a feeble resistance evacuated the first line of stockades, and retired to a second in the jungle.

The British followed up their first success, and totally unaware of the existence of this second line, suddenly blundered upon it and immediately kindled a panic among the enemy. Hundreds of the Burmese were bayoneted as they tried to escape, and the right division, even as the other two, was completely broken up.

So ended the last offensive movement of the Burmese Army, in rout and disgrace. The operations of the five days from the 1st to the 5th of December cost the British little over one hundred and fifty killed and wounded; but the merit of the troops must not be judged merely by the casualty-list. Fighting in close, steaming heat under a fierce tropical sun is very exhausting work, especially to Europeans who are not properly clothed for it; and we have no knowledge of the numbers which went into hospital in the course of these five days.

The men were worn out on the night of the 1st, yet they stormed the Napadi position on the 2nd; and there is something rather pathetic in the picture of this handful of weary soldiers, hardly one of them unweakened by previous sickness, toiling slowly for nearly three miles up and down rugged ridges with an occasional pause to clear out a stockade, taking no more notice of the enemy's bullets than if they had been rain-drops, but pressing on under the impetus of sheer discipline with the bayonet only, until the last entrenchment had been carried and the last wretched fugitive within reach had been despatched. By that time every stitch of their shabby scarlet must have been dripping with sweat as, choking with thirst, they threw themselves down to rest.

And then, when they fell in to march away to camp, the reaction would set in, and first one and then another would drop down with his teeth chattering, and there would be many cases for hospital next morning and possibly a grave or two wanted by the next night. But the worst was yet to come. Between the 6th and 8th of December, Campbell's division encamped on a plain eight miles north of Prome, with Cotton's at some distance to its left upon a road parallel to the river. The next objective was Meaday, and the enemy was known to have fortified a succession of positions between Napadi and that place.

Campbell was therefore to advance somewhat wide to eastward so as to turn all their positions, while Cotton, starting three days after him, was to follow the river with the flotilla, and meet him at Meaday. Campbell had still some hopes that Morrison would join with him from Arakan and Richards from Assam, not yet knowing that the one was paralysed by sickness and the other by want of transport. In Burma itself Campbell ordered Colonel Pepper, who was in charge of the garrison at Pegu, to advance upon Toungoo and distract the enemy upon that side; but Pepper, despite of the utmost exertion, could not obtain the transport that was essential to his movement. Campbell, therefore, whether he realised it or not, had to march to Ava alone.

On the 9th his column started, and for three days made its way northward along execrable roads without seeing a sign of man or beast. On the night of the 11th and during the whole of the 12th rain fell heavily, and the wretched paths through the jungle became impassable. The transport and the artillery were unable to move, and the way was choked with dead and exhausted cattle. Quantities of biscuit and rice were destroyed or damaged by the downpour, and the men, toiling painfully through dripping elephant-grass fifteen and twenty feet high, would have been no wetter if they had waded neck-deep in water. When the march ended, no open ground could be found but the dry bed of a rivulet surrounded by rank waterplants.

Next day cholera broke out, striking down the British right and left; and it should seem that for twenty-four hours the column was paralysed. On the 14th Campbell marched on, and emerging upon healthier ground halted for a day, when the plague began to abate. On the 16th he found traces of a hasty and disorderly retreat of the Burmese, and on the 17th he sent a cavalry patrol seven miles forward to reconnoitre Meaday. The patrol found the Burmese rearguard in the act of evacuating the last stockade; and on the 18th Campbell halted to await the junction of Cotton's column, which punctually arrived and brought cholera with it.

On the 19th the army entered Meaday, and then for the first time Campbell realised what was meant by a Burmese Army in rapid retreat. Alike within and without the stockades the ground was strewn with the dying and the dead, wounded soldiers who could drag themselves no farther, and helpless villagers, first driven from their homes to make a desert before the invaders and now left to perish of sickness and want. Newly made graves showed that the British advance had interrupted the work of burial; and the hideous remains of crucified victims gave grim evidence that the Burmese were enforcing their ruthless discipline to the last.

✶✶✶✶✶✶

Crucifixion with the Burmese signifies that the victim is tied hand and foot to bamboo formed into a St. Andrew's cross, that a splinter is thrust through his tongue to keep his mouth open, and that he is then left to the tender mercies of the flies. Examples were seen and photographed during the Burmese War of 1884-1885.

✶✶✶✶✶✶

The only sign of life came from huge packs of dogs and vultures, snarling and screaming at each other in the struggle for dainty morsels; and the stench was appalling. Campbell moved forward two miles on the next day in the hope of escaping from these horrors, but in vain. For fifty miles up the river and along the road by which the enemy had retired, the track of their retreat was marked by the same hideous tokens, and the air was tainted by the same foul breath of corruption. The very camping-grounds had to be cleared of corpses before the tents could be pitched. The villages had been burned or destroyed; the cattle had been driven off; no living men were seen except the dying; the once populous country was a solitary place. The Burmese host, like the Greeks before Troy, had become a prey for dogs and for the birds of the air.

On the 21st Campbell's division was obliged to halt, the supply of fresh beef for the Europeans having failed; and he continued the advance with the *sepoys* alone, moving painfully over infamous roads at the rate of six or eight miles a day. On the 26th, when about fourteen miles below Minhla, Campbell received a flag of truce from Ava; and, after moving forward for another ten miles, the column halted, while two officers went forward to that place to meet the Burmese negotiators.

As these last showed a disposition merely to gain time, Campbell broke off the parley and, having been joined by the flotilla on the 27th, moved up to Patanago, immediately opposite to Minhla, from whence he reconnoitred the Burmese position. It seemed to consist of a principal stockade, about a mile square, filled with men and mounting a number of guns, with outworks covering a total front, towards the river, of about two miles.

Under the stockades lay a large fleet of boats at anchor; and at the appearance of the British the crews rushed hastily to these craft and began to move them up the river. The British flotilla had not yet come up, being delayed by the intricacy of the navigation, but a few shots from the guns sufficed to stop the fugitives; and presently the *Diana* steamed up, passed by the stockade without the firing of a shot upon either side, and was received with honour by two gilded war-boats. These escorted her up the river and suffered her and her escorts to drop their anchors at some distance up the river, completely cutting off the retreat of the enemy by water.

Campbell accepted these conciliatory demonstrations with alacrity. The troops were halted; a truce was proclaimed; and it was arranged upon the suggestion of the Burmese, who can never have heard of the raft at Tilsit, that negotiators from both sides should meet in a boat moored in midstream between the two armies. Campbell wrote on the 31st:

> I earnestly hope that this is the last military despatch which I shall have to write upon the war in Ava.

And he sent down orders to the force at Pegu, forbidding for the present any further operations. The conference began on the 1st of January 1826; and after three days of hard bargaining a treaty was accepted and signed by the Burmese emissaries. Fifteen days, ending on the 18th of January, were allowed for ratification by the King of Ava, for the surrender of all British prisoners and for payment of an instalment of the indemnity, all of which formed part of the preliminary conditions. During this interval Campbell's Europeans came up; and there was friendly intercourse with the enemy, though it was noticed that the Burmese, despite of Campbell's remonstrances, persisted in strengthening their defences under cover of night.

The reason for this soon became apparent. On the 17th the Burmese emissaries reappeared to represent that, owing to some unknown accident, the ratification, the prisoners and the indemnity had not arrived from Ava. Campbell thereupon denounced the armistice. Hostilities began anew at midnight of the 18th, and before 10 a.m. on the 19th twenty-eight pieces of artillery were in battery ready to play upon the enemy's defences at Minhla.

At 11 a.m. they opened fire, and the troops were embarked,

three-fourths of them being designed to land above the place and attack the northern face, while the Thirteenth and Thirty-Eighth under Sale should disembark below the defences and assault the south-western angle. Owing to the strength of the current and a strong northerly breeze Sale's party reached its point of attack long before the other brigades; but, though Sale was himself wounded while afloat, his handful of men attacked without hesitation, entered the place by escalade and drove from ten to fifteen thousand Burmese before them. The other troops landed in time to strike in upon their retreat; and in a very short time the British were in possession of the stronghold of Minhla with all of its military supplies and stores, at a cost to the flotilla and the troops of some forty casualties.

As it happened, the enemy had suffered a sharp defeat in another quarter, during the armistice. Colonel Pepper at Pegu, having with much difficulty collected transport, began his advance towards Toungoo on the 23rd of December. Crossing the river at Myitkyo, where he had seized a number of native boats by surprise, he left there a post of one hundred and fifty men, and on the 3rd of January 1826 reached Shwegyin, about fifty miles north-east of Pegu, which, though strongly fortified, had been abandoned by the enemy.

This done, he, on the 6th, sent down a detachment under Lieutenant-Colonel Conroy of the Third Madras Light Infantry to capture the stockaded post of Sittang, about thirty miles down the river, so as to open communication by water between Shwegyin and Martaban. Conroy, proud of his *sepoys*, refused to take with him the Europeans that were pressed upon him by Pepper, and attacked the stockade on the 7th in full confidence of success. The Burmese, however, held their fire until their assailants were close upon them; and the *sepoys*, seized with panic at the first volley, ran back and would not be rallied. Conroy and another officer were killed, two more officers were wounded, and then there was a rush to the boats, and a hasty retreat by water to Myitkyo. The casualties, save in the matter of European officers, were trifling, not thirty men having been killed or wounded out of some five hundred present; and it is evident that the regiment behaved very ill.

The news of this mishap reached Pepper on the 8th, simultaneously with Campbell's letter announcing the armistice of the 30th of December and the consequent interdiction of further operations. Pepper ignored the letter, and on the 9th set out with some three hundred and fifty men, including eighty Europeans from Myitkyo. Here he spent the 10th in collecting boats, and embarking before dawn on the 11th came at 9 a.m. before the stockade of Sittang. This stronghold was situated on a knoll of steep ascent, built of stout teak timber from twelve to fourteen feet high, with square bastions to give a flanking fire, and was accessible only by fording a creek.

Pepper opened fire from his two pieces of artillery—a six-pounder and a light howitzer—and landing his little force, distributed it into three columns for assault at three different points. By 2 p.m. the tide had fallen low enough to enable the creek to be passed, though even so the men waded neck-deep, holding their ammunition-pouches over their heads; and at a given signal the three columns escaladed simultaneously. Once again the enemy held their fire until the last moment, and even the veteran flank companies of the Hundred-and-Second staggered for a moment before their first volley, while the native pioneers dropped the scaling-ladders and ran for their lives. But recovering themselves instantly, the white men climbed into the stockade; and then there was an ugly slaughter.

The troops had seen the corpses of Conroy and of their dead comrades hung, naked and foully mutilated, by the heels from a cross-beam, and were not inclined to be merciful. Over three hundred dead bodies were found within the stockade alone after the action, and it was reckoned that as many more had been carried off or hidden away. The loss of the assailants exceeded seventy, twenty-eight out of the seventy-two Europeans present having been killed or wounded—sufficient evidence that without them the attack would have failed once more.

The news of this affair, whether it reached the Burmese

Army in the north or not, seems to have produced little effect upon it. On the 25th of January, Campbell again moved forward by the worst roads and through the barrenest country that he had yet encountered. He was in fact approaching the district of petroleum wells, which do not make for fertility, and his cattle and horses were weak for want of forage.

In fact it had been found necessary to mount the troopers of the bodyguard upon ponies and privately owned animals, and to use officers' chargers to drag the guns of the horse-artillery, (Havelock). On the 31st he was relieved by the arrival at his headquarters of six British prisoners, who brought messages praying for peace and asking for the lowest terms that the British would grant. Re-stating the conditions which he had laid down in the negotiations before Minhla, Campbell continued his advance, and on the 8th of February was within a day's march of Pagan. Here he received certain information that the enemy was preparing to fight him under the walls of that city. Having been compelled to detach two brigades to gather in forage, he had no greater righting force than about thirteen hundred men; but this was sufficient; and he made his dispositions to attack on the morrow.

The march lay through jungle; and the advanced guard for some miles was constantly engaged in a running fight with small parties, until it debouched into an open plain, and came upon the Burmese Army, perhaps ten thousand strong, drawn up in the form of a crescent with the wings advanced. Campbell promptly attacked the two wings, on his right with the Thirteenth and four guns, supported by the Eighty-Ninth; on his left with the Thirty-Eighth and two guns, supported by the Forty-First; while his single *sepoy* battalion advanced on his extreme left by the river, to parry any turning movement of the enemy in that direction.

The resistance of the Burmese troops was feeble; but their general showed tactical insight, for he struck at once at Campbell's centre, which, to all appearance, was uncovered and was certainly very weakly held; and he made several attempts with his cavalry to turn Campbell's right. The spirit of his troops was, however, so poor that they were easily driven from their ground, and their counter-attacks were as easily checked. They appear, after losing their first position, to have rallied upon a second, for the fighting, such as it was, lasted for five hours and carried the British over some four miles of ground; but, as the British casualties amounted to no more than eighteen killed and wounded, the combat cannot have been very severe.

On the other hand, a party of three or four hundred Burmese who took refuge in a field-work was exterminated; and the bulk of the hostile army was utterly dispersed. The Burmese commander, returning to Ava with the tidings of his defeat, was by the king's order immediately put to death. This action was decisive. On the 13th two liberated British prisoners came in to the camp to announce that the King of Ava accepted Campbell's terms. As, however, there was still a disposition to haggle and to evade them, Campbell continued to advance, now entering, for the first time, a populous and well cultivated country. He had arrived at Yandabo, within forty-five miles of Ava, before a fresh embassy came in, bringing with them all British prisoners and twenty-five *lacs* of *rupees* as earnest of their good faith in conceding the British demands; and on the 24th of February the definitive treaty was signed.

Arakan and the Tenasserim provinces were surrendered for ever to the British government; and the King of Ava agreed to renounce all right of interference with Assam, Cachar, and Jaintra, and to recognise the reinstatement of the former Rajah of Manipur if that potentate should desire it. The king further consented to pay an indemnity of one million sterling; and it was covenanted that, upon discharge of one-fourth of this sum, the British troops should retire to Rangoon, and, upon the further discharge of the like proportion, should evacuate the Burmese dominions. It was stipulated finally that the king should receive a British minister at Ava and send a Burmese minister to Calcutta.

Fortunate it was that the court of Ava gave way when it did.

Had it remained resolute in its determination to defy the British, abandoned Ava and fled to the north, the position of the Indian Government would have been to the last degree embarrassing. The occupation of Arakan and of Burma from Ava southward, under constant menace of an attack from the north, would have been a burden in men and money too heavy to be borne, and, even if taken up for a time, must inevitably have been thrown off. Then the evacuation of the country would have meant not only that the effort spent upon the expedition had been wholly fruitless, but that the Burmese were unconquered and invincible.

In truth this first Burmese war went perilously near to be a disastrous failure. It was, beyond all question, forced upon the authorities at Calcutta; but it must be confessed that they were utterly outwitted by the court of Ava. Indeed the foresight and calculation shown by the Burmese leaders in formulating their military policy, and the tenacity with which they adhered to it, were very remarkable.

In principle that policy was nothing new, being exactly that which was followed by Wellington in Portugal from 1810 to 1812, and by Alexander in Russia in 1812; but never in the history of the world has it been more thoroughly enforced; and that it was so enforced, at untold sacrifices to the wretched villagers, is a high tribute to the court of Ava. That the government of that court was to the last degree tyrannical and ruthless is, of course, not to be denied; but there is none the less something grand in its strength and resolution.

The authorities at Calcutta had left such power and constancy of will in an indigenous enemy completely out of their calculations; and perhaps they may be pardoned, for these qualities are not commonly seen in such perfection. Who the moving spirit at Ava may have been, we know not. It may well have been that one and all of the dominant class were inspired by the same high contempt for the invaders and the same determination at all costs to drive them into the sea.

In any case, the result was the same. The government at Cal-

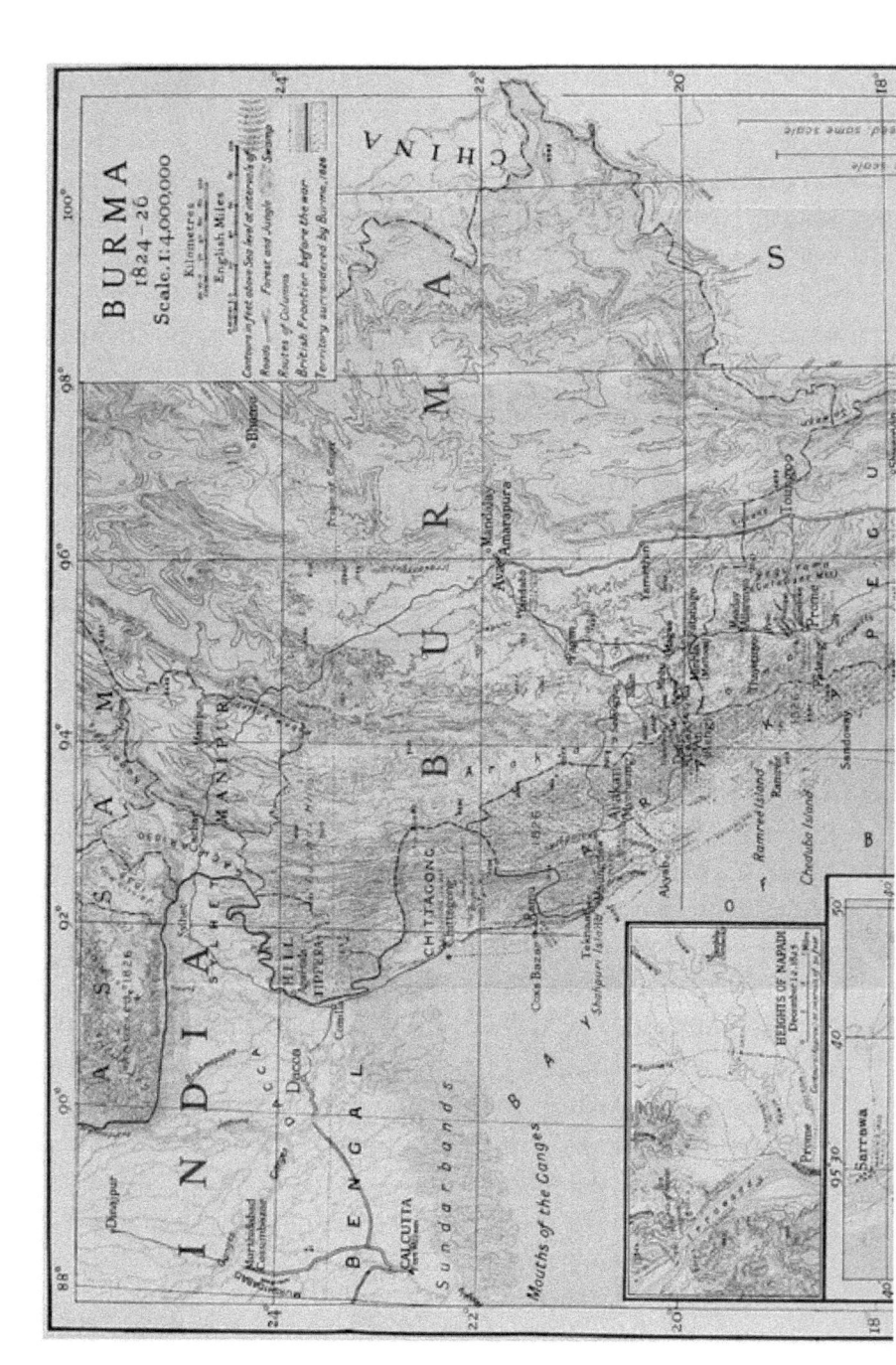

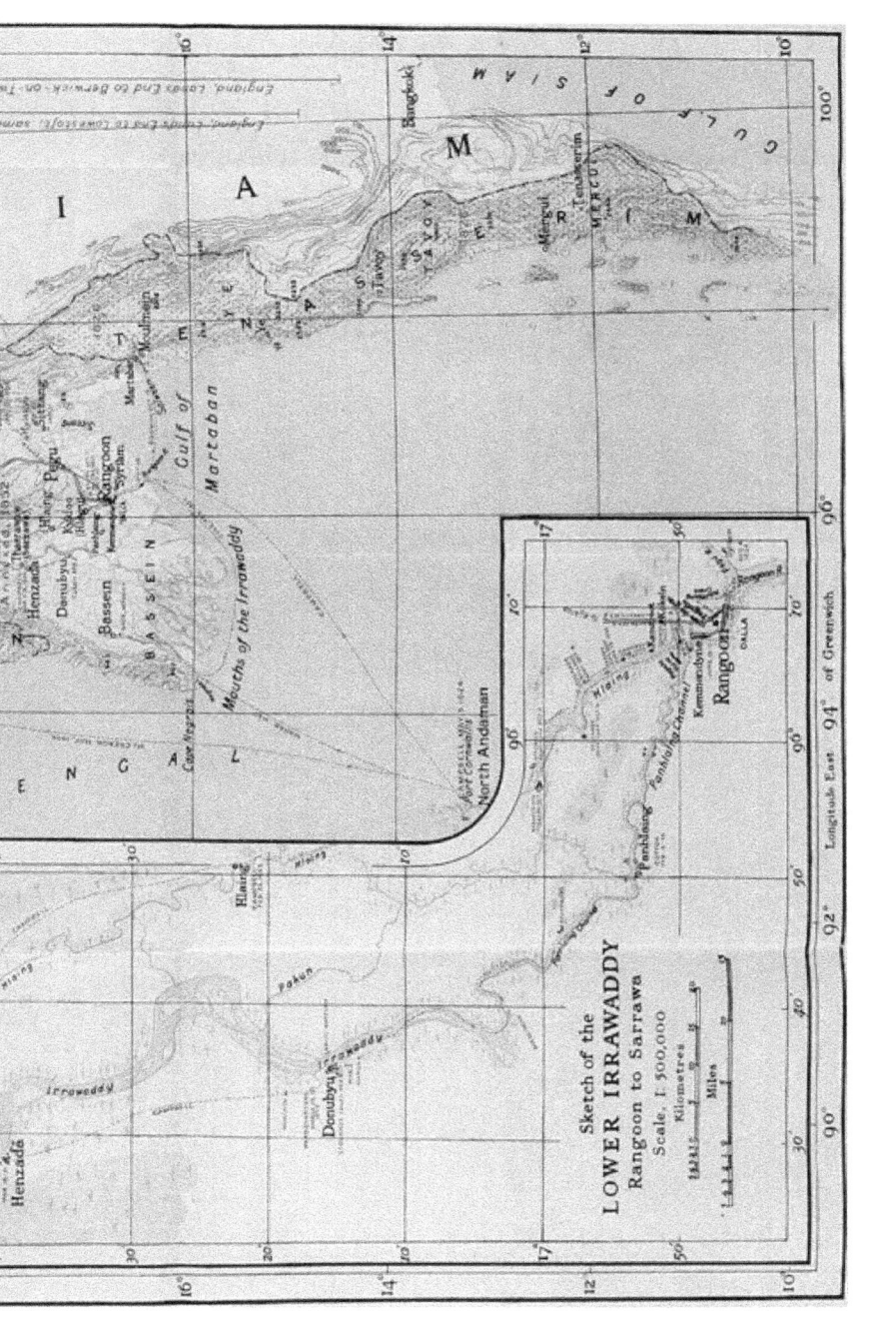

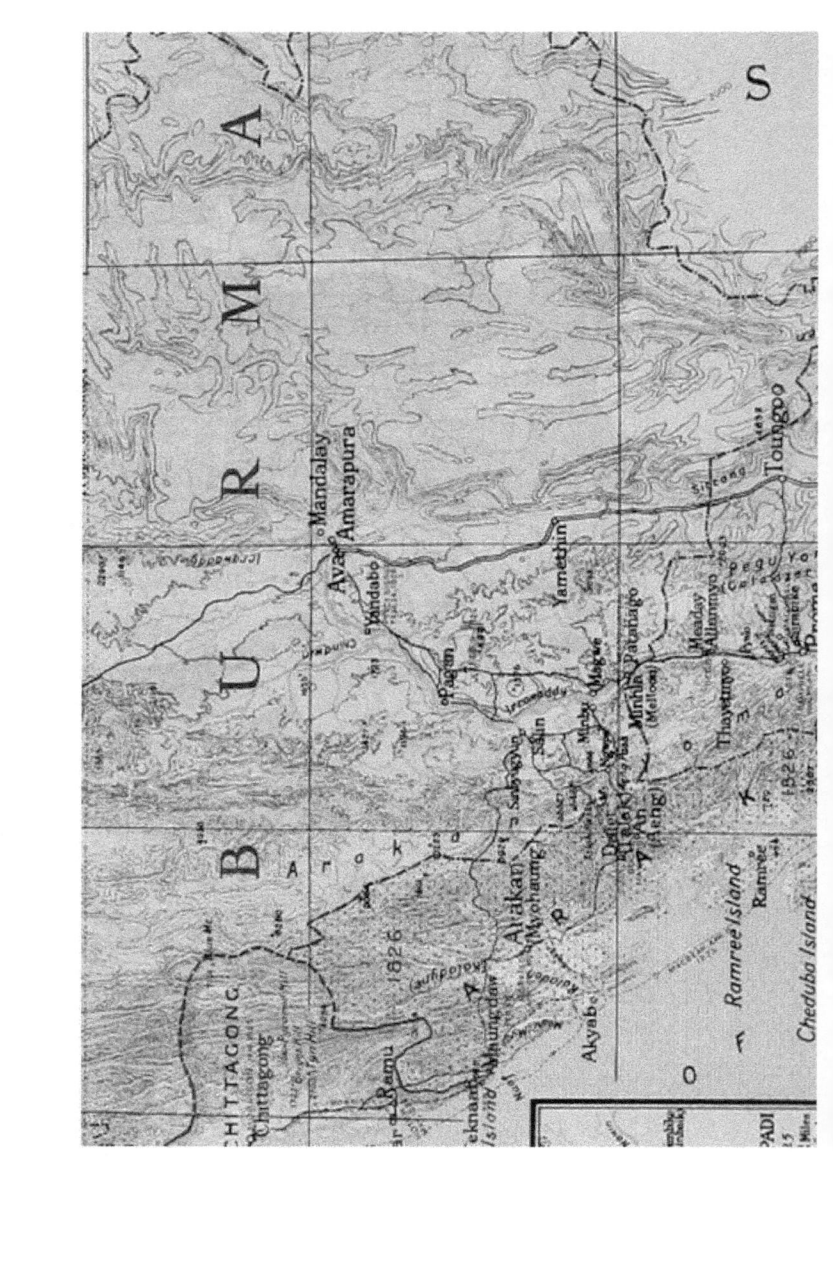

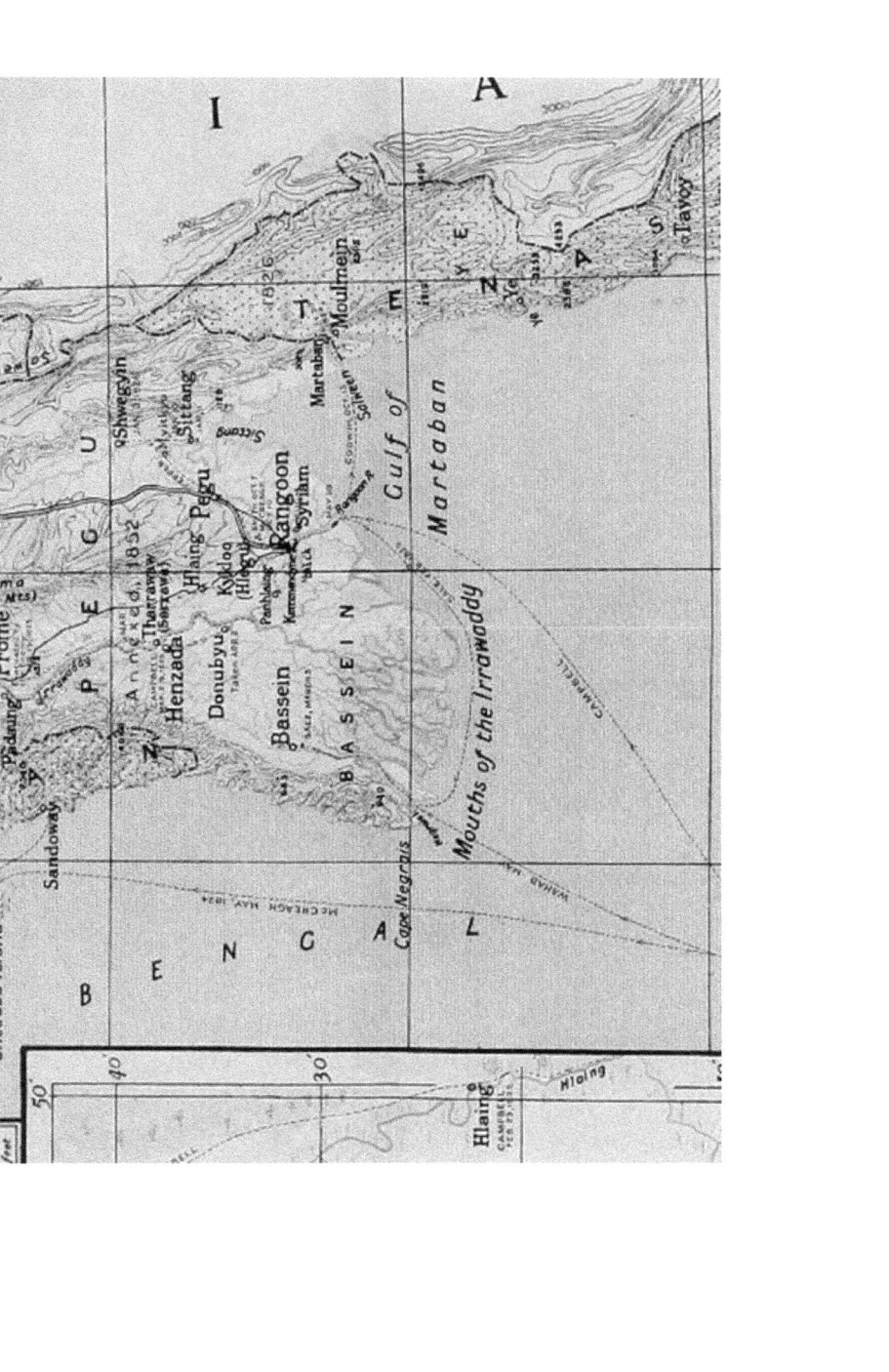

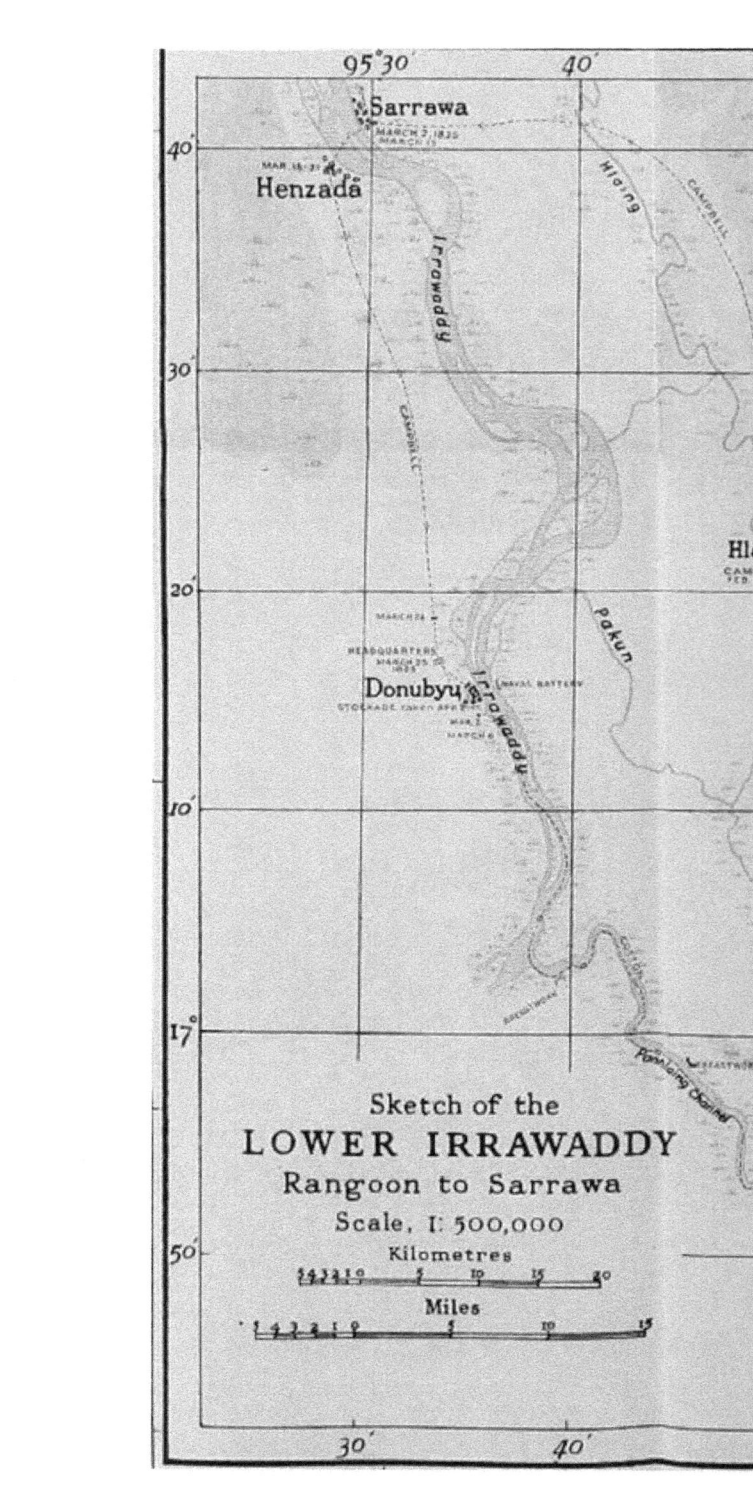

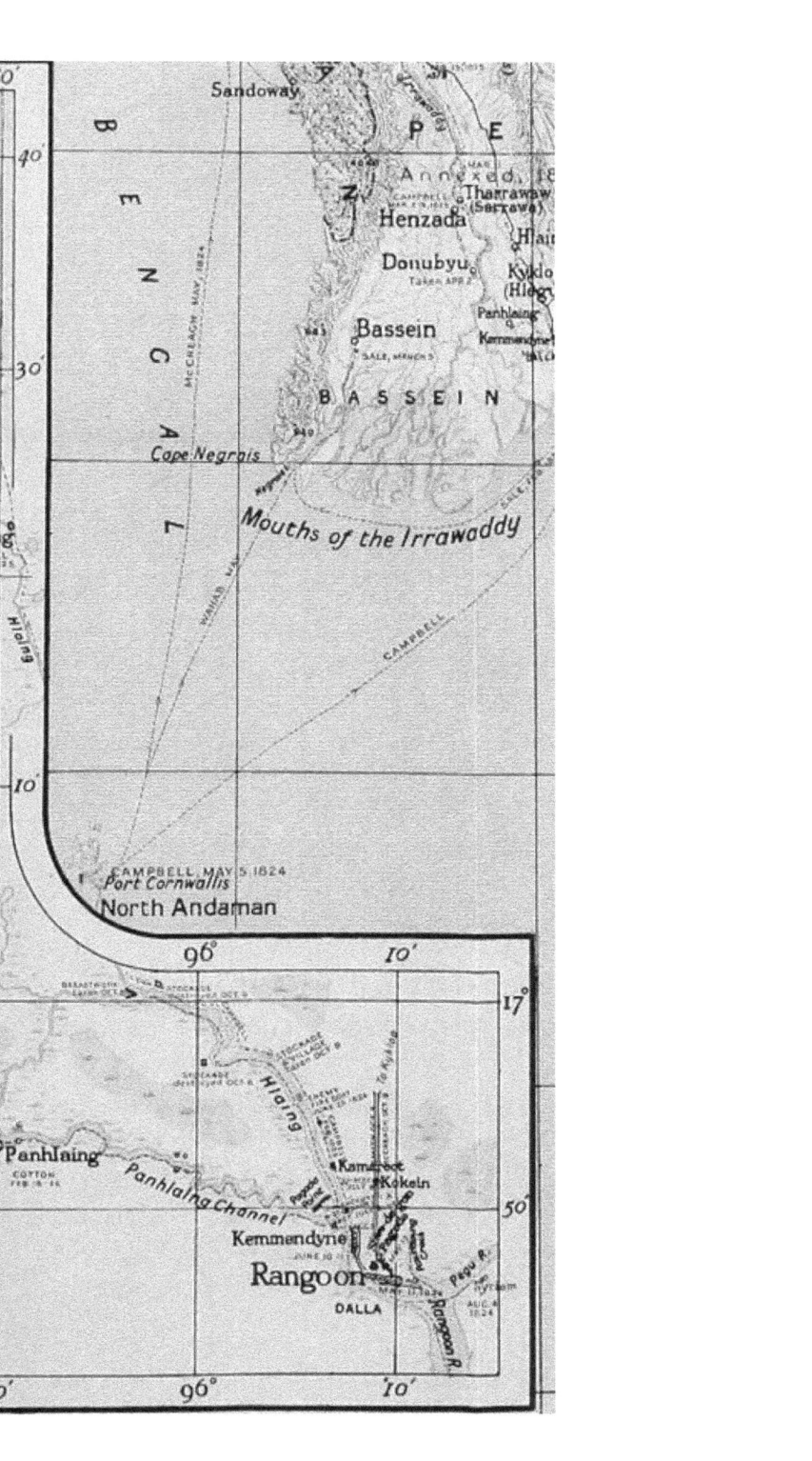

cutta was flustered and frightened. In its dread of the plagues that guarded for the Burmese the valley of the Irrawaddy, they sought to shorten the war by sending, upon very imperfect information, little columns to break into Upper Burma from the west and north, where the country was infinitely more difficult and the climate even more pestilential. Whether the authorities justly lie open to the old reproach of frittering away their force at several points instead of concentrating it at one is not so simple a question as might at first sight appear.

It is doubtful whether Campbell could have fed or transported a larger army, even if it had been furnished to him; and the case stands as a parallel to that of the Peninsular War in 1809, when Wellington frankly confessed that, if the troops despatched to Walcheren had been sent instead to Lisbon, he would have been unable to use them in the field. But the landing at Walcheren did at least stir Paris to its depths, whereas the diversion in Arakan and Manipur merely destroyed troops at great expense without contributing in the least to the relief of Campbell's difficulties.

Moreover the authorities, at any rate in Madras, continued to deal carelessly and neglectfully with the troops to the end. The remnant of the Hundred-and-Second, twelve officers and about two hundred men, together with over four hundred native followers, were all crowded upon a single transport of four hundred and fifty tons' burthen, for the return voyage, which, the south-west monsoon being at its height, occupied six weeks from Rangoon to Masulipatam. Hanging would have been none too severe punishment for the persons responsible for this wanton wickedness.

As to Campbell himself, it has already been remarked that he was not a man of sufficient originality or imagination to devise the means of meeting the Burmese tactics without a sharp lesson or two in the school of defeat. It must now be added that his despatches were absurdly magniloquent, and that they were not regarded by, at any rate, some of those who served under him, as very accurate.

★★★★★★

Butler's criticism must be discounted, as he was evidently sore because Campbell had not given to his regiment (the 102nd) the credit which Butler considered to be its due. Such things happen in every campaign, and too much must not be made of them. But in the copy of Wilson's *Papers* which I have used there are marks of exclamation against several passages of Campbell's despatches, evidently made by some one who knew the facts, which lend some countenance to Butler's comments.

★★★★★★

Lastly, although in the absence of fuller information it is unwise to pass final sentence, the deviation from his original plan, which brought about Cotton's reverse before Donobyu, does not appear to indicate a commander of sound and orderly judgment. But there is another side to the question which shows Campbell in a far more favourable light.

He was sent out with a very imperfectly equipped force to execute an extremely difficult task. For months his troops not only lacked every comfort, but were half starved and half poisoned, and were pent up within the lines of Rangoon. The mortality among them in those lines was appalling; and, even when they were at last set in motion, fever and dysentery accompanied them everywhere, giving place occasionally to the more terrible scourge of cholera. The five British regiments which originally landed at Rangoon, (H.M. 13th, 38th, 41st, 47th and 89th), numbered, exclusive of officers, something over thirty-five hundred; and of these there died over thirty-one hundred, not one in twenty of them from the weapons of the enemy.

★★★★★★

The actual figures are: strength, 3586; deaths, 3115. I have been unable to discover whether these regiments received any drafts. Possibly they may, at the very outside, have received 1000 men partly from home, partly from other regiments in India. The 102nd (Doveton) lost 600 out of 900 by action and disease, and certainly received no drafts.

★★★★★★

Of their officers, sixteen out of one hundred and fifty were killed or died of wounds, and forty-five succumbed to disease. The officers were obliged to dispense with all the little luxuries—really not far removed from necessities—which alone make life in the tropics bearable by the white man. It was not until the winter of 1825-1826 that they were able even to procure themselves ponies to ride upon the march, and transport sufficient to give them some little comfort.

Of course it is easy in theory to lay down the proposition that the officers should fare exactly as their men; but this ignores the fact that officers have to see to a great many things during the day's march and after it which, at the best of times, keep them continually on the move and abridge them of much of their rest. In this expedition, where the majority of the marches lay through jungle along narrow and tortuous paths, not unfrequently in pitchy darkness, the physical exertion required from unmounted officers in keeping the column together must have been excessive.

Moreover, it must be remembered that one officer in every three was always on the sick-list, which of course threw the more work upon the survivors and broke them down in turn. Practically every failure of the *sepoys* in an attack may be traced to the fact that, after the fall of the two or three British officers who were with him, there were no others to take their place. Never, probably, has the British officer been subjected to more long-continued hardship, privation and discomfort than in this campaign; and this he had to bear, not only without hope of glory, which he could easily have endured, but with little prospect of prize-money, which was the great attraction of Indian warring in those days.

The same, of course, is true of the men. Few British soldiers can have spent a more miserable year than those who landed at Rangoon in May 1824. Unsuitably clothed, vilely fed, imperfectly tended, drenched with rain when they were not bathed in sweat, eaten up by mosquitoes, leeches and the manifold other plagues of a tropical delta, they had literally nothing but misery and death before them. Active operations were their only relief; yet even here they were set to haul guns through marshes, and to do such heavy work as should not be demanded of white men in the tropics.

Moreover, their arms were not much better than those of their enemies, whom they were required to drive from jungle, stockades and entrenchments, which were all to their own disadvantage. It was solely through their discipline that they could meet the Burmese at odds of one against five; and that discipline never failed in the field or in garrison. When the inhabitants, free from the iron yoke of their masters, began timidly to creep back to Rangoon and to Prome, they were heartened not only by the perfect behaviour of the troops but by that irresistible good nature which the British soldier carries with him to every country and every climate from the Arctic circle to the equator.

Of course, as invariably happens and as was, in the circumstances, inevitable, they formed attachments closer than were warranted by mere good nature. Many a little Burmese girl dressed herself as a man and tried to sail to India in the transports; and not a few men, rather than forsake their too faithful mistresses, deserted and took service with the Burmese when the time came for them to leave the country. Nevertheless, on the whole, the conduct of the British soldier during this most trying campaign seems to have been exemplary.

We have seen British expeditions in the past fall to pieces when subjected to a similar ordeal. But this Burmese field-force, despite of all misfortunes, epidemics, hardships and privations, was never demoralised, always ready for action and full of dash and spirit in the field. For this, Campbell, as it seems to me, deserves no ordinary praise. It must be remembered that the Calcutta government, though itself mainly responsible for the prolongation of the war, was always clamouring for Campbell to end it. No doubt he himself was as anxious as the government itself to be quit of it; and frequently, even so early as December 1824, he flattered himself that his enemy would sue for terms. Yet it was not until he reached Prome that the court of Ava condescended even to play at negotiation; and from that time, September 1825, until February 1826 he was kept on tenter-hooks of expectation, and again and again disappointed.

The advance from Prome must have been a most anxious operation. The country was almost impassable; his line of communication was long; his transport-cattle dwindled steadily from overwork; disease inexorably dogged his footsteps; every day saw his force grow weaker and weaker. Upon leaving Meaday for the fifty miles' march through devastated country among the dead and dying villagers, the troops could with difficulty throw off the depression of their environment. A staff-officer, (Snodgrass), wrote:

> We appeared to traverse a vast wilderness from which mankind had fled; and our little camp of two thousand men seemed but a speck in the desolate and dreary waste that surrounded it.

They were but a handful, daily growing fewer, in the heart of a hostile country, marching upon a capital still two hundred miles distant, in defiance of an enemy that outnumbered them by ten to one and without hope of further reinforcement. To conduct such an enterprise, to keep all that share in it of good heart, and to carry it to a successful issue demands peculiar qualities in a leader; and no one, I think, can deny to Archibald Campbell an iron nerve, a strong will, high moral force and abundant moral courage.

Chapter 4

The Second Burma War

At the outbreak of the Afghan war, and at every critical period subsequent to that time, the Indian Government had been harassed with the apprehension of trouble in Burma. It was evident that the Court of Ava was rapidly forgetting the lessons of 1826. The treaty of Yendabo provided for the protection of British merchants at Rangoon, and the king even agreed to receive a British resident at Ava. But two successive residents were treated with such indignity that it was decided to withdraw the British representative; and therewith there began oppression of British merchants and trading captains at Rangoon, rising to such a height that in 1851 the governor-general, Dalhousie, demanded the removal of the governor of Rangoon and an indemnity for the injured British subjects.

The Court of Ava answered on the 1st of January 1852, in terms of seeming compliance. A new governor was sent to Rangoon, and the old one was allowed to return in triumph to Ava; but the new governor soon proved himself to be even worse than the old. He offered a deliberate insult to the British flag, which he declined to redress at the protest of the Commodore of the British squadron in the Irrawaddy; and the situation became so dangerous that on the 6th of January the commodore ordered all British merchants and residents in Rangoon to repair on board his flagship, seized a Burmese vessel as a pledge for the satisfaction denied to him, and declared the mouths of the Irrawaddy to be in a state of blockade. On the 9th he towed his prize-vessel down the river.

The Burmese war-boats followed him, and fire was opened upon his ship from Burmese stockades. Therewith three vessels of war cannonaded the stockades for two hours, sank one large war-boat, and having wrought much destruction and killed, as was reported, some three hundred Burmese soldiers, passed down the river and made for Calcutta.

Dalhousie's first measure was to reinforce the garrisons of the Tennasserim provinces and Arakan, and he then ordered the commodore to return to Rangoon and demand an apology. The ships were fired upon as they went up the river. Further negotiations came to naught, and in the middle of February Dalhousie resolved to send a military expedition to Burma. It was limited in the first instance to a brigade from Bengal and another from Madras, the whole under the command of Major-General Godwin, who had served in the first Burmese war in command of the Forty-First Foot. The lessons of that war were not wholly forgotten.

A stockade was erected at Dumdum to test the effect of artillery fire upon such an obstacle; the Eightieth Foot received practical instruction in the work of escalade; and since the majority of the war-vessels and some of the transports were steamers—not only paddle-steamers but screw-steamers—the task of ascending the Irrawaddy could not but be much easier. The time chosen for the enterprise differed materially in 1852 from that of 1824. In the latter year the season of the monsoon had been preferred, so that there should be abundance of water in the Irrawaddy. The expedition of 1852 was timed to arrive at the beginning of April, about six weeks before the breaking of the rains.

The Bengal contingent was the first to arrive at April, the mouth of the Rangoon River on the 2nd of April, the Madras contingent following four days later. Godwin and Admiral Austen, the naval commander-in-chief of the station, sailed on the 3rd with the Bengal troops for Moulmein, the capital of the British Tennasserim provinces, and on the 5th attacked Martaban, over against it on the Burmese border. The place was strongly fortified, but the guns of the war-vessels sufficed to break down all resistance, and the few troops landed were practically not engaged. On the afternoon of the 8th the Bengal contingent returned, and Godwin for the first time had his entire force under his hand, (see list following), altogether close upon six thousand men, rather fewer than half of them Europeans.

Bengal Infantry Brigade.
      H.M. 18th, H.M. 80th; 40th B.N.I.
Madras ,,   ,,
      H.M. 51st; 5th, 9th and 35th M.N.I.
2 companies of Bengal Artillery.
3 ,,   ,, Madras ,,
2 ,,   ,, Madras Sappers and Miners.

April is the hottest month of the year in Burma, and cholera had already made its appearance, which was disquieting, (Laurie, *Rangoon*, 1852); and, as the Burmese had long been active in fortifying Rangoon, it was evident that no time must be lost in beginning operations before the rains should set in. Accordingly on the 11th five war-steamers proceeded up the river and cannonaded the stockades upon both banks, utterly destroying those upon the left bank, where a magazine was blown up, and kindling those at Dalla on the right bank by the help of a small landing-party of seamen and marines. The Burmese batteries answered the ships, and several vessels were struck by their shot; but the damage done was not serious and the casualties were insignificant. Thus all was made safe for a landing, which was appointed to take place on the following day.

Since 1824 there had sprung up a new Rangoon about a mile north of the river. It was of quadrate form, very nearly a mile square, and surrounded by a ditch, abatis and a mud wall, the last about sixteen feet high and eight feet broad. At the northeastern angle stood the Shwe-da-gon Pagoda, which, with its enclosures, had been worked into the general scheme of the defences as a citadel. It was known that over twenty guns, some of them of large calibre, had been mounted in this citadel, and the strength of the entire Burmese garrison was reckoned at twenty thousand men; so that, if the enemy should make any resistance at all, there might be serious work at hand. All previous experience, however, promised an easy conquest, which was the more probable since the place was within fairly close range of the heavy guns and rockets of the ships.

Under cover of their fire the troops landed early in the morning of the 12th, and were formed into two columns, the Eighteenth, the Fifty-First and the Fortieth Bengal Native Infantry, with four guns on the right, a wing of the Eightieth and the Ninth and Thirty-Fifth Madras Infantry on the left. Godwin moved off with the right column before the left was landed, fetching a compass so as to attack the eastern front of the citadel. He had not gone far when he was checked by artillery-fire from a stockade, known as the White House stockade, on his right front, while simultaneously Burmese skirmishers appeared in the jungle on his flank.

These last were easily driven off, but the four guns fired away all their ammunition at eight hundred yards' range with no great effect, and not until two twenty-four-pounder howitzers had played for some time upon the stockade were four companies of the Fifty-First and the Madras Sappers ordered to carry it by escalade, which they did with little loss.

Far more serious than the Burmese fire was the effect of the sun, which prostrated many men and was fatal to at least two officers. Godwin, therefore, decided to advance no further. The engineers burned the White House stockade, so as to render it untenable, and the troops bivouacked for the night six hundred yards to south of it, without molestation save for a single harmless volley of Burmese muskets.

Throughout the hours of darkness the ships continued to bombard the camp, and the greater part of the garrison seems to have seized the opportunity to quit it. The troops halted on the 13th, thankful for the rest owing to the intense heat, while the bluejackets toiled all day, landing four heavy howitzers and dragging them up to the bivouac. About seven o'clock on the morning of the 14th the march was resumed, the advanced party being four companies of the Eightieth with four guns. These cleared away the Burmese skirmishers from the jungle and enabled the guns to get into position; but it was not until 10 a.m. that the heavy howitzers were brought forward, and meanwhile the fire of the Burmese artillery caused some little loss.

At 11.30 the storming-party was formed of four companies of the Eightieth, two of the Eighteenth and two of the Fortieth Bengal Native Infantry, which advanced across a hollow for about half-a-mile upon the eastern face of the *pagoda*. The hill on which it stands was divided into three terraces, upon all of which guns were mounted, but there was a long flight of steps in the centre of these, and for this the storming-party made a rush. The Burmese gave way at once, and, before the main body could come up, the *pagoda* was taken. Its fortifications proved to be even stronger than had been expected.

First came the ditch, then ten yards of abatis with a stout paling in the middle of it, then a row of great tree-trunks, three deep and touching each other, set vertically, then another barrier of tree-trunks laid horizontally, and finally a bank of earth tapering from forty-five feet of breadth at the base to twenty-four feet at the top. The guns captured in the entrenched camp numbered ninety and the wall-pieces eighty, and there was a vast quantity of ammunition. Yet the operations of the three days from the 12th to the 14th of April cost no more than seventeen of all ranks killed and one hundred and thirty-two wounded, the casualties of the Eighteenth, which suffered more heavily than any other corps, not exceeding forty-six.

The losses of the fleet did not amount to twenty men.

Then followed a period of inaction with its inevitable result of an increase of sickness, the heat being intense, and cholera still abroad. Within the next month more than fifty men of the Fifty-First died, and the Forty-Ninth Native Infantry had at one time three hundred men in hospital. Happily, the Burmese soon lost their fear of their enemies, and refugees speedily returned to Rangoon to work for them and to run up houses for them against the breaking of the rains. The bazaar, too, was well supplied with fresh fish, poultry and vegetables, so that there was no fear of the scurvy, which had been such an affliction to the British troops in Rangoon in 1824.

On the 7th of May four or five hundred men were sent up the river in three steamers, and on the 8th disembarked for a march of seven miles inland, in the hope of catching the fugitive Burmese governor of Rangoon; but the expedition proved to be fruitless, and the troops suffered very greatly from the sun. On the 12th the Sixty-Seventh Bengal Native Infantry arrived to reinforce Godwin, and on the 17th he embarked about eight hundred men, half of them of the Fifty-First, on three steamers, and proceeded with them and with a fourth steamer carrying a naval brigade, to Bassein.

Descending the Rangoon River and ascending the Negrais, the flotilla passed along the whole length of the defences of Bassein, and at 4 p.m. on the 19th anchored over against their higher end without the firing of a shot. The troops were landed at once, and nearly half of them were ashore before the Burmese at last opened fire, when the flotilla answered with all their guns. A single company of the Fifty-First sufficed to storm a pagoda which was the centre of the Burmese defences on their right, and the bulk of the force was turned against a mud-fort of considerable strength on their left. Both were carried with little difficulty, while simultaneously the Naval Brigade assaulted and captured a fort upon the opposite bank.

In less than an hour the whole affair was over, and Bassein, together with eighty-six guns and wall-pieces, fell into Godwin's possession. The casualties did not exceed twenty-three of all ranks, of whom two natives only were killed, and fifteen, including four officers, were claimed by the Fifty-First. On the 23rd Godwin returned to Rangoon, leaving five hundred troops to hold Bassein, which Archibald Campbell had styled the Key of Burma.

The next incident was an attack of the Burmese upon Martaban at dawn of the 26th, which was repulsed without difficulty and with considerable loss to the enemy, whose retreat was cut off by gunboats sent up the river to Salween. Godwin then turned his attention to Pegu, the inhabitants of which had risen in insurrection against the Burmese; and on the 3rd of June two companies of infantry, with a few sappers and miners, seamen and marines, started up the river in boats towed by the steamer *Phlegethon*. The party seems to have gone to work in a very casual fashion, for next morning the military landed upon one bank, hearing the sound of firing between the Burmese and Peguese, and the naval contingent, under Commander Tarleton, on the other.

Leaving no guard in charge of the boats, Tarleton marched inland after a body of Burmese, failed to overtake them, was fired upon from some ruined walls as he returned, drove the enemy from them, and then discovered that a party of Burmese had pounced upon his boats and plundered them. The military commander, having also intelligence of this, hurriedly marched back to the river, and the two forces returning to the boats recaptured them, and then gave their men rest until the afternoon.

While they were thus halted a party of Burmese came down upon them, but took to their heels on being attacked; and the old town of Pegu was captured, after a travesty of a fight which did not cost twenty lives to both of the parties engaged. The place was made over, for political reasons, to a native garrison, which in a week or two was driven out by the Burmese, so that the whole expedition was an absolute futility.

The operations had now been proceeding for three months. The Burmese had been defeated in every encounter; Martaban, Rangoon and Bassein had been occupied; the Irrawaddy was straitly blockaded; and it was expected that the Court of Ava would show signs of submission. Since none were forthcoming, Commander Tarleton was sent up the Irrawaddy with five steamers to examine the defences of Prome. He did his work well, eluded the Burmese army that was awaiting him by taking his ships up an unusual channel, and, reaching Prome on the 9th of July, found it without a garrison.

Having no troops, he could not occupy the city, and was fain to return, having wrought such destruction as he could among the defences of the place and the Burmese war-canoes, but accomplished, through no fault of his own, nothing more substantial than a bold and thoroughly successful reconnaissance. It does not appear, however, that any blame can be attached to Godwin. The native battalion which reached him in May may have made good his losses through action and disease, but no more. He had but six thousand men, a large proportion of them in hospital, (at Martaban the sick numbered 40 *per cent* of the strength), distributed in three different stations, and it would have been imprudent to disperse them still further by throwing a garrison into Prome. The Burmese might be a contemptible enemy, but they had, as had been seen in the former war, a quick eye for an exposed or isolated detachment, and they had the climate on their side.

On the 27th of July the governor-general, Lord Dalhousie, arrived at Rangoon to examine the situation for himself, and, having decided that the operations must be conducted on a larger scale, returned on the 1st of August to Calcutta. On the 25th he issued orders for the augmentation of the force to two divisions, with a total strength of about twenty thousand men, (see list following), and there was great activity at Rangoon in the preparation of a flotilla of transport-craft and armed boats, and in further fortification of the Shwe-da-gon Pagoda.

Bengal Division: Brig.-General Sir John Cheape.

1st Brigade: Col. Reignolds, H.M. 18th.
    H.M. 18th; 40th and 67th N.I.

2nd Brigade: Lt.-Col. Dickinson, 10th N.I.
    H.M. 80th; 10th N.I.; 4th Regt. Sikhs.

3rd Brigade: Lt.-Col. Huish, 37th N.I.
    101st (Beng. Europeans); 37th N.I.; Ludhiana Regt.;
    1 Light Field-battery.

Madras Division: Brig.-General S.W. Steel.

1st Brigade: Col. Elliott, H.M. 51st.
  H.M. 51st; 9th and 35th N.I.

2nd Brigade: Brig.-Gen. McNeill.
  102nd (Madras Europeans); 5th and 19th N.I.

3rd Brigade: H.M. 84th; 30th and 46th N.I.
  Sappers and Miners; 1 troop Horse Artillery;
  3 cos. Foot Artillery.

The reinforcements began to arrive in September; on the 16th and following days Reignolds's brigade was embarked for Prome; and on the 25th Godwin embarked likewise, Admiral Austen having already gone ahead in a steamer. The flotilla assembled on the 27th in Panhlaing Creek, and proceeding up the river arrived before Prome on the 9th of October, before which day the naval command had, through the admiral's death on the 7th, devolved upon Commodore Lambert.

As the steamers approached, the Burmese opened fire with guns and musketry, which was quickly silenced by the war-vessels. The flotilla then anchored; a few troops were landed on the same evening and had a slight brush with the enemy; and, when the remainder disembarked on the following morning, it was found that the enemy had evacuated the town, and fallen back upon their main body, said to be eighteen thousand strong, ten miles east of Prome. Godwin decided not to make any movement against them until Elliott's brigade, which had already received its orders, should have joined him. As this brigade could not move until the flotilla had descended the river to Rangoon, it was not until November that the last of it was embarked; and meanwhile Godwin returned to Rangoon, leaving Cheape in command at Prome.

Godwin's next enterprise was to lead a second expedition, made up of detachments of the Hundred and First, Hundred and Second and Madras Fusiliers, together about one thousand strong, to the capture of Pegu. These troops embarked on the 19th of November, anchored a little below Pegu at sunset of the

20th, and landed at five in the morning of the 21st in dense fog. The river at this point was only one hundred yards wide and so shallow that the war-vessels could give no assistance; but a couple of heavy howitzers were disembarked, and the advance began.

The Burmese, of course, looked for an attack upon the eastern wall facing the river, so Godwin decided to assault the southern wall, which involved a march of about two miles through grass, breast-high, and very dense jungle. The troops had hardly entered it when the Burmese opened fire from all sides and maintained it continually. Godwin called forward a working-party to clear a track, pushing out a company of native infantry to cover them; but the work took long, and meanwhile the men became much scattered.

For more than four long hours they floundered on under an incessant rain of bullets in stifling heat, with the sun blazing down upon them. At last the leading files, with Godwin at their head, emerged opposite a gateway which was the appointed place of assault; but the men were too much exhausted to move further. With great difficulty about two-thirds of the Europeans were collected, and, after a short rest, were urged on by Godwin to the assault. With the first rush resistance, as usual, collapsed at once, and by 1 p.m. Pegu was in Godwin's possession at a cost of fewer than fifty casualties.

But the fight, to judge by the accounts of those who took part in it, was a blind and unpleasant affair, (Laurie, *The Second Burmese War*), for nothing could be seen except occasional puffs of smoke, nor heard, except the whistle of bullets and the roll of musketry; no one knew very clearly what was going on, and it was difficult to convey orders to any officer, for no one could say where he was to be found. Had the enemy been Kafirs or Ashantis the result might have been disastrous; but with the Burmese it was safe to take almost any risk.

Leaving two hundred of the Hundred-and-Second, and as many native infantry with two guns, under command of Major Hill to garrison Pegu, Godwin on the 22nd returned with the remainder to Rangoon. Hardly was his back turned when, at nightfall of the 24th, the Burmese made an unsuccessful attack upon the gunboats lying off Pegu. On the 27th they assailed not only the gunboats, but also the pagoda which formed the citadel of Pegu, in both cases without success.

On the night of the 3rd of December they renewed their onslaught on the garrison, and on the night of the 5th they intercepted a commissariat-boat, guarded by twenty-four *sepoys*, which was on its way up the river from Rangoon, burned the boat and captured all but two of the guard, who brought the news to Pegu. Hill sent out a party to the river, which rescued the survivors without difficulty; but on the morning of the 6th the enemy closed in upon the pagoda in great force and thenceforward held it besieged under continual fire both day and night.

Meanwhile the commodore, learning the fate of the boat sent up on the 5th, despatched Commander Shadwell, with six armed boats on the 8th, to reopen communication with Pegu. On the 10th Shadwell reached the landing-place, but found it defended by large bodies of Burmese, and after losing thirty-two killed and wounded—about one-fourth of his strength—was fain to return to Rangoon for reinforcements. Meanwhile urgent messages came in from Hill reporting that he was hard pressed and that his ammunition was running short; but unfortunately two of the river-steamers needed repair and could not be made ready until the 11th.

On that night Godwin embarked thirteen hundred men upon them and upon a flotilla of boats, and at daylight of the 12th the whole started for the Pegu River. On the 13th there also left Rangoon a column of four hundred *sepoys*, a battery of horse-artillery and a troop of irregular horse, which was ordered to march upon Pegu by land under the command of Lieutenant-Colonel Sturt of the Sixty-Seventh Native Infantry. The flotilla reached its appointed landing-place, some five miles below Pegu, on the afternoon of the 13th, and the troops were disembarked in the course of that evening and the following morning.

At 7 a.m. they moved off in two divisions, the advance consisting of four hundred of the Hundred-and-First and Hundred-and-Second, three hundred Sikhs, and two ship's guns dragged by blue-jackets under Godwin in person, and the reserve of four hundred of the Hundred-and-First and two hundred Madras *sepoys* under Brigadier-General Steel. Marching inland Godwin manoeuvred to strike upon the eastern face of the pagoda, so as to take the besieging force in rear, and, beyond a little bickering with skirmishers, encountered no opposition. His casualties were no more than a dozen killed and wounded, but, by the time that the day's work was over, the troops were utterly exhausted by the heat.

However, the renewal of desultory fire by the enemy in the afternoon compelled the clearance of his defensive works on all sides, and the men could not settle down for the night until after dusk, when they took such cover as they could against the damp and the drenching dew. The force had left Rangoon, owing to the urgency of the case, in the lightest possible order. Not an officer, excepting Godwin and Steel, had a horse. The men had brought with them the least possible amount of clothing, and many, having no greatcoats, suffered bitterly from cold, making them an easy prey to fever and dysentery.

On the morning of the 15th a force of nine to ten thousand Burmese was observed entrenching itself some four miles to northward, and Godwin, who had never yet brought his enemy fairly to action, was anxious to defeat it decisively and break it up. He wrote significantly, bearing in mind the elusiveness of his foes:

> But, I cannot state how far I can go, as the progress of all soldiers depends upon feeding them, which can never be left to accident.

The truth is that the question of land-transport presented as serious difficulties in 1852 as in 1824. Dalhousie fully recognised the fact, but had been unwilling to face the enormous expense of providing land-transport except in case of absolute necessity, (Laurie). Nor were there wanting plenty of superficial critics, who maintained that the campaign could be carried to a decisive issue with water-transport only. But an army that could not leave the Irrawaddy was as powerless as a fleet for inland operations. The enemy had only to retire three days' march from the river in full confidence that the British could not follow them further, and advance again at their leisure when the British returned to their boats.

During the autumn of 1852 Dalhousie, alive to this important fact, ordered two hundred elephants to be sent from Assam and the borders of Arakan over the Aroka mountains into the valley of the Irrawaddy, and so to Prome. But these had not yet arrived, and meanwhile Godwin had to be content with eighteen buffalo-carts, which with great difficulty he had procured at Pegu.

On the 17th accordingly he marched northward at 7 a.m. with about twelve hundred men, (101st, 570; 102nd, 150; 10th B.N.I., 182; Sikhs, 330; Sappers and Miners, 30), each man carrying his greatcoat and one day's cooked provisions, while the bullock-carts carried supplies for six days. Passing through the jungle to the north of Pegu, the force emerged into an open plain and came within sight of the enemy's entrenchments, which were in three lines, extending from the river for a mile to the eastward.

Godwin manoeuvred to turn their left, being their unprotected flank, but by the time that he had formed his columns of attack the Burmese were in full retreat. He followed them up for ten miles to a large village, where the men found good quarters for the night, but not a living soul, and, what was worse, not a grain of corn. On the 18th he advanced yet another ten miles to another village, where the Burmese made some show of resistance but speedily retired; and on the 19th the state of his supplies compelled him to return to Pegu.

On that same day Sturt's column entered Pegu after a march of seventy-two miles, in the course of which he had found all the people not only friendly but helpful. Not an enemy of any kind was seen, though there were signs that they had but lately quitted a tract of dense jungle some five miles to south of Pegu. Sturt reported that artillery- or baggage-waggons having once entered the narrow tracks in this jungle, could not escape destruction at the hands of a resolute enemy which, if attacked, would be perfectly safe from pursuit. He added that he had found abundance of fine bullocks within fifteen miles of Rangoon; but this was of no great help to Godwin, for Rangoon, as he said, was the one place where he did not want them. Where he did want them was at his outlying posts, and particularly at Prome.

In truth it was evident that these outlying posts, if the garrisons had no power, from want of transport, to take the offensive, were sources of weakness and almost hostages given to fortune. They furnished vulnerable points against which the Burmese, whether regular troops or gangs of *banditti*—dacoits, to use the familiar native name—could wage an incessant petty war of attrition by harassing picquets, assassinating sentries, cutting off unwary individuals who ventured out too far from the lines of defence, and in particular by constant night-attacks which meant wearing exertion to officers and men.

At Prome these tactics seem to have been followed by the enemy throughout November, and they culminated in a serious attack, which was repulsed at every point, at the end of the month. Fatigue, of course, signified sickness, and privation of fresh provisions, milk and vegetables yet more sickness. The moral effect of passive endurance, forced upon the men, was perhaps more damaging to their health than even fatigue and privation. Then again communication by water could not be called safe. The steamers could take care of themselves, though always subject to "sniping" fire from the banks; but smaller craft, if they ran aground or were caught in some channel, which the Burmese had staked, could be and were occasionally overpowered by the enemy.

Altogether, the situation was by no means quite comfortable; and Godwin, while relieving Pegu and reinforcing the garrison, was anxious, throughout the whole of his operations there, to hasten to Prome. It was his own fault that he had been distracted to Pegu at all, for he had certainly left too small a garrison there in the first instance; and it was significant that, immediately upon his return from Pegu on the 20th of December, the Burmese reassembled and invested the place once more. Without land-transport it was difficult to see how he could strike any effective blow against the Burmese forces in the field.

A new series of operations was forced upon him by a proclamation of the governor-general on the 20th of December, annexing the province of Pegu. This document announced that all Burmese troops should be driven out; and accordingly a column was organised under General Steel to march through the province from end to end. Its strength amounted to rather over two thousand men, (1 co. Sappers and Miners, 1 co.—European—Madras Artillery; 101st, 450; 102nd, 150; 4 cos. 10th B.N.I.; 4 cos. 5th M.N.I.; 3 Rifle cos. M.N.I.; detachment of Irregular horse), six hundred of them Europeans, with four heavy howitzers, four light mortars and rocket-tubes.

The commissary at Moulmein had managed to collect in the Tennasserim provinces one hundred and twenty elephants, three hundred bullock-carts with teams, and some hundreds of spare bullocks, so that Steel was able to start with one month's supplies. Since his destination, Toungoo, lay one hundred and eighty miles as the crow flies from his point of departure, Martaban, and the navigation of the Sittang River was uncertain, Steel directed another month's provisions to be sent up by water to Pegu. Having taken this precaution, set out from Martaban on the 14th of January 1853.

His march being practically bloodless and unopposed, it need be mentioned only that he reached Shwegyin on the 12th of February, where he found a certain quantity of supplies, which had been brought up the Sittang in boats, awaiting him in the river. He received also intelligence that the provisions which he expected from Pegu were being sent forward to Myitkyo. The headman at Shwegyin, being friendly, furnished sixty boats;

and Steel, embarking ten days' supplies upon these, and loading as much again upon elephants and bullocks, started on the 15th with nine hundred men for Toungoo, which was surrendered to him upon his approach on the 22nd. There he halted to await orders from Godwin, after a march of two hundred and forty miles through unknown forest. Though recent traces of the Burmese Army were noted at many stages, he had actually seen no enemy.

Godwin, meanwhile, repaired on the 29th of December to Prome, which he reached on the 5th of January. He was met by the news that the Burmese forces had vanished. There had been a revolution at Ava, and all armed men were hastening thither to share in the spoil. Accordingly on the 23rd he proceeded up the river to Meaday, while Sir John Cheape led a column to the same place by land.

A new stockade of most elaborate construction was there found—empty—and on the 27th there arrived a deputation from the prince who had displaced the old King of Ava, with a message which pointed to negotiations for peace. Godwin returned a peremptory answer, and, leaving a garrison of five hundred men at Meaday, returned to Prome. The rest of the land column, under Sir John Cheape, likewise returned to Prome on the 3rd of February, where Cheape found that there was more serious work before him.

The national army of the Burmese might find full employment for itself in supporting or opposing those who had rebelled against the old King of Ava; but the *banditti*, or *dacoits*, were working actively upon their own account, and the most formidable of these were a gang which worked under the leadership of one Myat-Toon of Donubyu. Ever since the opening of the war this chief had been a thorn in the British side. He was always on the watch for the British boats as they passed up and down the river, and, pouncing upon any that were careless or unwary, had captured several.

With a force reckoned at seven thousand men he laid waste the country of the people friendly to the British, and towards the end of 1852 had carried his ravages to within thirty miles of Rangoon, finally settling down at Donubyu.

On the 17th of January 1853, a flotilla of armed boats attempted to penetrate up a narrow creek leading to Myat-Toon's stronghold and was driven back with some little loss. It was then determined to send a stronger force against him, consisting of about two hundred and fifty seamen and marines and three hundred of the Sixty-Seventh Bengal Native Infantry, with two light guns, the whole under command of Captain Loch of the Queen's ship *Winchester*. Leaving Rangoon in the first days of February, Loch brought his flotilla up to Donubyu, and, finding all the creeks running inland to be staked and impassable by boats, decided to disembark and march upon Myat-Toon's stronghold by land.

Accordingly he struggled forward for several miles through the jungle, and when within two miles of the hostile stockade was turned by his guide into a narrow path. Following this with his whole force he found himself checked by a deep, wet ravine, and came to an abrupt halt. He could not go on; he could not, owing to the dense jungle, turn to right nor left; and before he could turn back he found himself under a very heavy fire from the front and both flanks. Loch and two more officers were mortally wounded almost at once, whereupon the senior military officer, Major Minchin of the Sixty-Seventh Bengal Native Infantry, took command, formed a rear-guard, and brought the remnant back after an exhausting retreat to Donubyu. The mishap was due entirely to the neglect of all military precautions, as was to be expected when the movement was not under the direction of a military man.

No attempt was made to reconnoitre the path before the entire column was committed to it; and it is evident that the whole of the Europeans were in front, for they lost fifty-nine killed and wounded, whereas the *sepoys* in rear lost but twenty-three. Had the enemy been really formidable they would have destroyed the party to a man, for they did their best to cut off its retreat; and on the whole, bad and inexcusable as the whole affair was, it might have been a great deal worse. All of the wounded were brought off, though the two guns were spiked and abandoned; and Godwin pointed the moral by issuing an order that in all expeditions by land the senior military officer should take command of all naval officers irrespective of rank.

It was to avenge this misfortune that Cheape was summoned from Prome, taking with him about seven hundred and fifty picked men, more than half of them of the Eighteenth and Fifty-First, with two guns and some rocket-tubes. His force was landed at Henzada, some thirty miles north of Donubyu, where bullock-transport was obtainable; and, his information being that Myat-Toon's stockade was three or four days' march distant, he started on the 22nd, with eight days' supplies, designing after his work was done to re-embark at Donubyu.

For four days he marched through the jungle, only twice seeing any sign of an enemy; and then, believing himself to be still far from his destination and having no intelligence except that the way thither was barred by an unfordable creek, he turned back to the river. He reached it at Zooloom on the 28th, and, moving part of his force by land and part by water, arrived at Donubyu on the 3rd of March.

Here he was lucky enough to surprise a Burmese picquet, and to take three prisoners whom he impressed as his guides. On the 6th reinforcements of five hundred men, one-fourth of them recruits of the Eightieth, joined him, also two mortars and a large supply of provisions. After leaving his sick and a small garrison at Donubyu, he was able to start again on the 7th with about a thousand infantry, half European, half *sepoys*, a hundred sappers and gunners, three rocket-tubes, four light pieces and a troop of irregular horse. Being assured that Myat-Toon's stronghold was within three marches, he took with him a week's supplies.

The way lay due west, and after traversing seven miles Cheape halted for the night, having arrived at the bank of a creek one hundred yards broad. Throughout the hours of darkness the Burmese kept up a dropping fire on the bivouac which did little damage; and the whole of the 8th was occupied in taking the column across the creek in two rafts, which Cheape had brought with him. On the 9th the march was resumed. No sign of any human being was encountered; and, the guide being mistrusted, another guide was chosen, who, after a long circuit under a blazing sun, brought the troops back to their original starting-place.

Cheape pushed forward a small advanced party for a mile; which surprised a party of the enemy; and the rest of the column, following, bivouacked on the bank of a creek fifty yards wide. The crossing of this obstacle occupied the whole of the 10th; and on the nth, after two miles of march, the column entered dense forest. There was some firing by the enemy both in front and rear, causing eight or ten casualties, and the enemy had felled trees across the track, which caused much delay. Late in the afternoon the force crossed a piece of water, and then the advanced party discovered that the guide had once again been at fault.

Every soul was so utterly wearied out that Cheape was fain to halt where he stood. Darkness fell long before the last of the bullock-carts came up; and the situation was so perilous that Cheape forbade the lighting of any fire. The night, however, passed off without disturbance from the Burmese, though a far more formidable enemy, cholera, made its appearance; and on the 12th the column retraced its steps to the ground which it had occupied on the 10th. The troops were thoroughly depressed; Myat-Toon seemed to be undiscoverable; and there had been thirteen deaths from cholera.

As provisions were running short, Cheape thought it prudent to put the men on half-rations, and sent back his bullock carts with an escort of three hundred men to fetch further supplies from Donubyu. Meanwhile he could only remain halted, with cholera striking men down right and left, and a few Burmese bullets flying into camp every night.

On the 16th the convoy returned, and on the afternoon of the 17th an advanced party set out again on the old road, carried a breast-work which the Burmese had thrown up across it, and sent back a prisoner who gave useful information. On the 18th, therefore, Cheape advanced at daybreak, leaving his sick, wounded and surplus provisions under a small guard, encountered another breast-work late in the afternoon, carried it with small loss, and halted for the night on the bank of a creek.

Pushing on early on the 19th he came upon another muddy creek with a breast-work beyond it, and knew that he had found his quarry at last. Bringing up his guns to engage the enemy in front, he decided to pass round the head of the water-course and attack the breast-work by a path leading into it on the enemy's right. The Eightieth and Sikhs led the attack, but were met by so heavy a fire that they were repulsed. They then tried to find a way round the right flank of the breast-work, but were stopped by dense jungle and abatis.

The Eighteenth then came up, but were likewise beaten back with severe loss. The enemy's fire of grape and musketry was, in fact, so heavy that unless it could be quelled, it seemed impossible for any storming-party to reach the breast-work alive, for the path was not only swept from end to end from the front, but also enfiladed by a flanking work. Cheape therefore brought up a twenty-four-pounder howitzer, and, pushing out skirmishers to cover its advance, opened fire from it with canister at a range of twenty-five yards.

The gun's crew naturally suffered for their temerity, but the Burmese suffered more. The remnant of the defeated parties was rallied, with Ensign Garnet Wolseley of the Eightieth at their head; and fresh men were brought up from the Fifty-First and from the Sixty-Seventh Bengal *sepoys*. The whole then advanced with a rush, carried the breast-work, and, falling to work with the bayonet, scattered the defenders with very heavy loss.

Myat-Toon escaped; and, though Cheape at once despatched troops to his village, neither there nor on the road thither was a living soul to be seen. All of the chief's resources were within his stockade, and it was reckoned that he had four thousand men—about four men to every yard of its length—to defend it.

But all were dispersed, and his power was broken. By the 24th Cheape and his column had returned to Donubyu with their work done.

Rarely have British troops been more severely tried than in this little campaign of twenty-four days; and it says much for Cheape's tenacity that he was able to hold them together through all their trials, disappointments, hardships and privations. Forest-fighting against an invisible human enemy under a tropical sun is hard enough, but, when the living foe has cholera for his ally, the combination is very formidable. The casualties in the actual assault numbered ninety-five, among the hurt being young Garnet Wolseley, the future field-marshal and commander-in-chief, who, having his thigh ripped up by a *jingal*-ball, was crippled for life as a horseman, though he walked without a limp. The killed and wounded in the whole expedition amounted to one hundred and thirty, and the deaths from cholera exceeded one hundred, altogether an appreciable loss in a party of no more than eleven hundred and fifty of all ranks.

This was the last serious action of the war. After some negotiation the Burmese accepted the cession of the province of Pegu as the price of peace, and the cessation of hostilities was finally proclaimed on the 30th of June 1853. There was some little trouble in that province owing to an abortive insurrection in April 1853, and again in the opening months of 1854, but order was restored with little difficulty or loss, and the details are no better worth recounting than those of a hundred petty affairs of police in the Indian Peninsula. Nothing therefore remains to be added to the narrative of the Second Burmese war.

It is noteworthy that the press both in England and in India was very impatient in its criticism of Godwin for the slowness and prudence of his operations; and as he was not a young, though he was an exceedingly active man, he was set down as too old for his work. It should seem that shallow observers, dazzled by the rapid development of steam-vessels, and by the dash and enterprise manifested by naval officers in the handling of the same, deemed it a simple matter for a flotilla to ascend the river to Ava with—or even without—a sufficient body of troops, and to dictate terms to the Burmese court there and then.

The fallacy is an old one, and it may not be amiss to expose it even for the hundredth time. Water-craft, whether armed cutters or battle-ships, cannot work ashore. Again and again the navy has tried to do work of both services, but has invariably failed. Duckworth sailed up the Dardanelles in 1807 with little difficulty, but was glad, when he sailed down again, to escape with considerable loss; and, if the fleet had succeeded in forcing the passage of the same strait in 1915, it might have undergone the same experience.

Now a river is, from a naval point of view, nothing more than a long strait. It may not be very difficult to go up, but it is impossible to keep the passage open for the downward journey without a chain of military posts on the banks. The garrisons for such posts devour a military force very rapidly; they are themselves a source of anxiety, being always open to attack by a sudden concentration of the enemy; and, unless furnished with some proportion of land-transport, they cannot sally out and break up the enemy's bands in detail before concentration is accomplished.

Moreover, in such a climate as that of Burma, where thirty to forty *per cent* of the men may be in hospital, they may at times be almost powerless even to hold their own. In any case they must be supplied with food and ammunition, and possibly also with forage, which throws a great strain upon the resources of the navy. Where, as on the Irrawaddy, hardly a mile of the banks could be considered to be permanently free of an enemy, every convoy practically demands protection. Boats may creep up stream safely by daylight but must make fast to the bank for the night, and then comes the enemy's opportunity, as was shown, not unfrequently, in the course of this war. The loss of a boat or two from time to time may seem to be of no great moment, but if the craft happen to contain ammunition to supply a post which is hard beset, then it may be a very serious matter.

Moreover, the navy has its own technical difficulties. Ma-

The Capitulation of the Burmese

chinery needs constant attention and repair, and the boilers of 1852 were not so trustworthy as those of the present day. A breakdown of engines may mean days of delay, or even, at the worst, the loss of a vessel and a temporary paralysis of movement by water. Then there are the mischances which may, in spite of all skill and forethought, arise from shifting shoals, changing channels and falling waters; and the Burmese, being alert to multiply these mischances by art, and endless trouble by the staking of creeks and similar devices. A very little thought will show that headlong dashes of flotillas up the river would have been simply madness.

Dalhousie seems to have trusted mainly to the naval blockade to bring the court of Ava to reason, and he was not wrong, though it was obvious that the process would take time. Godwin's original force was not really strong enough to do much more than hold Rangoon and Bassein for the safety of the blockading vessels; and he cannot be blamed if he declined, until reinforced, to advance to Prome and Pegu. His enemies were everywhere, for though large bodies of the people were friendly, these were always subject to intimidation by dacoits, and could not, therefore, be counted upon. If he wished to make even Rangoon and Bassein absolutely safe, he must clear the country for some distance to northward upon all branches of the river; and this he could not do without land-transport.

We have seen how Dalhousie, after some hesitation, decided at last to furnish him with this transport from Assam and Arakan; and the march of the three hundred elephants to Prome was an incident which might furnish material for a romantic chapter. The Burmese laid their plans to intercept them by erecting a stockade near the entrance to the Aeng pass, but on the night of the 6th of January 1853, this stockade was surprised and captured by the Arakan local levies under the British officers, and thus the way was made safe.

The elephants finally crossed into the valley of the Irrawaddy by a pass a hundred miles south of Aeng, and the first of them came into Prome in the earliest days of March. It is significant that in those very days Cheape was groping his way through the jungle a hundred miles below Prome, in order to make secure the line of communication by the river.

Dalhousie's preparations, to his great relief, were rendered superfluous by the revolution at Ava, which no doubt was directly attributable to the blockade. Any further movement northward became unnecessary when the Burmese troops were already streaming thither of their own motion; and this was fortunate, for Prome must have been the advanced base, and the place was hideously unhealthy. Even as things were, scores of British soldiers found their graves at Prome.

Speaking generally, the hardships of the campaign were not comparable to those endured by the troops in the first Burmese war. The men were well fed and, according to the standards of the time, well looked after; but the exhaustion caused by any military operation in tropical jungle and swamp was inevitably excessive, and fever, dysentery and cholera claimed hundreds of victims. Such, however, is the work which the British expect as a matter of course from the British soldier; and, in accordance with the precedent set by Ellenborough in 1841, and followed by his successors after the Sikh wars, it was rewarded by a medal—that medal which, among a vast number of clasps issued during the long reign of Queen Victoria for service in the Indian Empire, includes one with the name of Pegu.

ALSO FROM LEONAUR
AVAILABLE IN SOFTCOVER OR HARDCOVER WITH DUST JACKET

THE 9TH—THE KING'S (LIVERPOOL REGIMENT) IN THE GREAT WAR 1914 - 1918 *by Enos H. G. Roberts*—Mersey to mud—war and Liverpool men.

THE GAMBARDIER *by Mark Severn*—The experiences of a battery of Heavy artillery on the Western Front during the First World War.

FROM MESSINES TO THIRD YPRES *by Thomas Floyd*—A personal account of the First World War on the Western front by a 2/5th Lancashire Fusilier.

THE IRISH GUARDS IN THE GREAT WAR - VOLUME 1 *by Rudyard Kipling*—Edited and Compiled from Their Diaries and Papers—The First Battalion.

THE IRISH GUARDS IN THE GREAT WAR - VOLUME 1 *by Rudyard Kipling*—Edited and Compiled from Their Diaries and Papers—The Second Battalion.

ARMOURED CARS IN EDEN *by K. Roosevelt*—An American President's son serving in Rolls Royce armoured cars with the British in Mesopotamia & with the American Artillery in France during the First World War.

CHASSEUR OF 1914 *by Marcel Dupont*—Experiences of the twilight of the French Light Cavalry by a young officer during the early battles of the great war in Europe.

TROOP HORSE & TRENCH *by R.A. Lloyd*—The experiences of a British Lifeguardsman of the household cavalry fighting on the western front during the First World War 1914-18.

THE EAST AFRICAN MOUNTED RIFLES *by C.J. Wilson*—Experiences of the campaign in the East African bush during the First World War.

THE LONG PATROL *by George Berrie*—A Novel of Light Horsemen from Gallipoli to the Palestine campaign of the First World War.

THE FIGHTING CAMELIERS *by Frank Reid*—The exploits of the Imperial Camel Corps in the desert and Palestine campaigns of the First World War.

STEEL CHARIOTS IN THE DESERT *by S. C. Rolls*—The first world war experiences of a Rolls Royce armoured car driver with the Duke of Westminster in Libya and in Arabia with T.E. Lawrence.

WITH THE IMPERIAL CAMEL CORPS IN THE GREAT WAR *by Geoffrey Inchbald*—The story of a serving officer with the British 2nd battalion against the Senussi and during the Palestine campaign.

AVAILABLE ONLINE AT www.leonaur.com
AND FROM ALL GOOD BOOK STORES

ALSO FROM LEONAUR
AVAILABLE IN SOFTCOVER OR HARDCOVER WITH DUST JACKET

ESCAPE FROM THE FRENCH *by Edward Boys*—A Young Royal Navy Midshipman's Adventures During the Napoleonic War.

THE VOYAGE OF H.M.S. PANDORA *by Edward Edwards R. N. & George Hamilton, edited by Basil Thomson*—In Pursuit of the Mutineers of the Bounty in the South Seas—1790-1791.

MEDUSA *by J. B. Henry Savigny and Alexander Correard and Charlotte-Adélaïde Dard*—Narrative of a Voyage to Senegal in 1816 & The Sufferings of the Picard Family After the Shipwreck of the Medusa.

THE SEA WAR OF 1812 VOLUME 1 *by A. T. Mahan*—A History of the Maritime Conflict.

THE SEA WAR OF 1812 VOLUME 2 *by A. T. Mahan*—A History of the Maritime Conflict.

WETHERELL OF H. M. S. HUSSAR *by John Wetherell*—The Recollections of an Ordinary Seaman of the Royal Navy During the Napoleonic Wars.

THE NAVAL BRIGADE IN NATAL *by C. R. N. Burne*—With the Guns of H. M. S. Terrible & H. M. S. Tartar during the Boer War 1899-1900.

THE VOYAGE OF H. M. S. BOUNTY *by William Bligh*—The True Story of an 18th Century Voyage of Exploration and Mutiny.

SHIPWRECK! *by William Gilly*—The Royal Navy's Disasters at Sea 1793-1849.

KING'S CUTTERS AND SMUGGLERS: 1700-1855 *by E. Keble Chatterton*—A unique period of maritime history-from the beginning of the eighteenth to the middle of the nineteenth century when British seamen risked all to smuggle valuable goods from wool to tea and spirits from and to the Continent.

CONFEDERATE BLOCKADE RUNNER *by John Wilkinson*—The Personal Recollections of an Officer of the Confederate Navy.

NAVAL BATTLES OF THE NAPOLEONIC WARS *by W. H. Fitchett*—Cape St. Vincent, the Nile, Cadiz, Copenhagen, Trafalgar & Others.

PRISONERS OF THE RED DESERT *by R. S. Gwatkin-Williams*—The Adventures of the Crew of the Tara During the First World War.

U-BOAT WAR 1914-1918 *by James B. Connolly/Karl von Schenk*—Two Contrasting Accounts from Both Sides of the Conflict at Sea During the Great War.

AVAILABLE ONLINE AT **www.leonaur.com**
AND FROM ALL GOOD BOOK STORES

www.ingramcontent.com/pod-product-compliance
Lightning Source LLC
Chambersburg PA
CBHW021010090426
42738CB00007B/730